REAL LOVE

REAL LOVE

The Truth About Finding Unconditional Love

and Fulfilling Relationships

GREG BAER, M.D.

GOTHAM BOOKS

GOTHAM BOOKS
Published by the Penguin Group
Penguin Putnam Inc., 375 Hudson Street, New York, New York 10014, U.S.A.
Penguin Books Ltd, 80 Strand, London WC2R 0RL, England
Penguin Books Australia Ltd, 250 Camberwell Road, Camberwell, Victoria 3124, Australia
Penguin Books Canada Ltd, 10 Alcorn Avenue, Toronto, Ontario, Canada M4V 3B2
Penguin Books (N.Z.) Ltd, 182–190 Wairau Road, Auckland 10, New Zealand

Penguin Books Ltd, Registered Offices: Harmondsworth, Middlesex, England

Published by Gotham Books, a division of Penguin Putnam Inc.

First printing, January 2003
10 9 8 7 6 5 4 3 2 1

LIBRARY OF CONGRESS CATALOGING-IN-PUBLICATION DATA

Baer, Greg.
    Real love : the truth about finding unconditional love and fulfilling relationships / by
Greg Baer.
        p. cm.
    ISBN 1-59240-000-0 (alk. paper)
        1. Man-woman relationships. 2. Interpersonal relations. I. Title.

    HQ801 .B1155 2003
    306.7—dc21

                                                                        2002026072

Printed in the United States of America
Set in Adobe Garamond with Diotima Display

CONTENTS

v

4 Taking the Leap of Faith: Everyday Wise Men and How to Find Them 63

Remember the Wart King · Being Patient: Don't Expect Brass Bands · Having a Desire to Change · Exercising Faith · Telling the Truth About Yourself · Giving Up the Getting and Protecting Behaviors

5 The Effect of Real Love: Like Money in the Bank 117

Real Love Is Like Money in the Bank · The Effect of Real Love on the Past and the Present · Real Love: The Answer to All Our Relationship "Problems" · The Need for Consistent Real Love · Magnifying the Effect of Real Love with Gratitude

6 Sharing Your Fortune: The Power of Loving Others 136

Loved: We Can't Give What We Don't Have · Seeing: The Elimination of Our Own Blindness · Accepting: The Natural, Peaceful Result of Seeing · Loving: Caring About the Happiness of Other People

7 Playing a Beautiful Duet: The Joys of Mutually Loving Relationships 170

Telling the Truth About Ourselves · Telling the Truth About Our Partner · Telling the Truth All the Time · Making Requests · Working Things Out · Faith in Mutual Love · Becoming One

ACKNOWLEDGMENTS

This book is the result of a learning process that involved un-counted thousands of steps, most of which I'm sure I don't appreciate or remember. I can't possibly acknowledge the contribution of everyone who taught me about love and rela-tionships, but I can at least make a feeble attempt to do that. I feel a profound sense of gratitude that I'll never be able to fully express

- to those I inconvenienced and injured. We learn by mak-ing mistakes, and perhaps I chose that avenue more than most. I learned about loving and relationships by making mistakes that caused pain and hardship for many people who had hoped for much better from me.
- to those who loved me. I can only repay them by sharing with others what I've learned.
- to those who allowed me to practice on them while I was learning. All the material in this book was field tested on brave souls who were willing to try what I suggested.
- to my wife, Donna. I never imagined feeling as uncondi-tionally loved by one human being.
- to my children, who patiently allowed me to make innu-merable mistakes as a parent while I learned how to love them.

I'm also grateful to those who were so helpful in the development and production of the book itself:

- to my literary agent, Wendy Sherman, who has expressed an energetic faith in me and held my hand through the publication process.
- to Bill Shinker and Lauren Marino at Gotham Books, who had the vision to develop this idea.
- to Judy Kern, who taught me that being an author doesn't necessarily make one a writer.

INTRODUCTION

Like most of us, I was told as a child that if I did all the right things—set my goals high, worked hard, and followed the rules along the way—I would accomplish great things. And it was further implied that, as a result, I would grow up to be happy. All our lives, we've heard people declare that they'd be happy *if only* they had more money, or a better job, or more sex, or a bigger house, or more opportunity to travel, or something else. I was determined to ensure my future happiness by having an abundance of all those things and more, and from an early age I worked hard to earn them.

I was valedictorian of my high school class, finished college in two and a half years, and received the highest honors in medical school. After completing my internship and specialty training in eye surgery, I eventually established one of the most successful ophthalmology practices in the country. I performed thousands of operations and taught other physicians locally and across the country. I was a leader in my church and in the local Boy Scouts organization. I had everything money could buy, and I was a husband and the father of five beautiful children.

By the time I reached my late thirties, I'd accomplished almost every goal I'd ever set for myself, but despite all my successes, I slowly came to the terrible realization that I had not achieved the happiness I'd been promised. When I was standing in front of a group of physicians, teaching the latest surgical techniques, and everyone was admiring me for my knowledge, I felt relatively satisfied with my life for the moment. And some of those expensive vacations were exciting while I was actually in those far-off, exotic places. But when I was all alone, with nothing to distract me, I knew something was missing—I just didn't know what it was. I couldn't have worked any harder. I'd done everything I'd been assured would bring me the happiness I wanted, but still something was wanting.

I found it difficult to sleep at night and began to take some of the sleeping pills we kept at the office for postsurgical patients. When those were no longer effective, I took other tranquilizers, and before long I was injecting narcotics every night. I rationalized my drug addiction for a long time, but it increasingly affected my behavior and my emotional health. Then, one evening, as I sat in the woods behind my house with a loaded Smith & Wesson 10mm semi-automatic pressed to my head, I finally realized that I couldn't rationalize my behavior any longer. I knew I needed to do something about my life.

I went to an in-patient drug treatment facility, and after my discharge I participated in several twelve-step programs for a while. Getting off the drugs saved my life, but it only put me back where I'd been when I started using them. I was still desperately missing something, but this time I was determined to find out what it was. I tried individual and group therapy, support groups, men's groups, New Age techniques, and Native American spiritual groups, among others. Each had wisdom to offer, but the old emptiness I felt was not being filled.

In my searching, I found many others whose feelings were similar to mine. Most of them hadn't been addicted to drugs, but they all were missing the profound happiness they'd always hoped for in their lives. We began to meet together in our homes, where we tried a variety of techniques I'd experienced or read about. Gradually, we eliminated the things that didn't work, and we discovered some principles that were astonishingly simple and effective. People who had been unhappy for a long time, in many cases despite years of therapy, were finding the first genuine happiness they'd ever known.

As we began to figure out what worked, I started writing down what we'd learned, handing out a few pages at a time to the men and women who participated in those early "experiments." Eventually, my observations became two self-published books that have now been read by thousands. I've shared these principles with people all over the country, and as they've applied them, their lives have changed in remarkable ways.

When I was trying to fill my emptiness, and later, as I was learning to change my life, I made many mistakes as a person, a husband, and a father. Among other things, those mistakes caused the end of my twenty-two-year marriage. Learning—as I discovered—can be very expensive. Now I'm deeply gratified to see the results of what I've learned, and to share it all with you. My second wife and I are the parents of seven children between us, and we're happier than we'd ever imagined it was possible to be.

Certainly there is a demonstrated need for people to learn something different. Half the marriages in this country end in divorce. One out of three children is now raised in a single-parent home. Ten to twenty percent of us are addicted to alcohol or drugs. One third of all girls and forty-five percent of all boys have had sex by age fifteen (compared with five percent for girls in 1970 and twenty percent for boys in 1972). Twenty-one percent of ninth graders have had four or more sexual partners. Nine percent of adult males will spend some time of their life in prison. I believe those statistics provide overwhelming evidence that we're unhappy and looking for something that's missing in our lives. Thousands of people have found that "missing something" as they've implemented the principles in this book. And I have great confidence that you, too, will enjoy the same experience.

REAL LOVE

1

The Missing Ingredient

What Relationships Really Need

Relationships fail all around us every day—between spouses, lovers, siblings, friends, and co-workers, among others. But despite an abundance of self-assured finger-pointing, the people involved rarely have any idea what actually went wrong. As a result, many people seem to be caught in an endless cycle of disappointment and unhappiness, blindly repeating the same mistakes.

Lisa came to see me because she was having problems with her fiancé, Doug. It was obvious that she was angry at him. "We met almost a year ago," she said, "and we fell in love right away. I knew he was the one for me. We never spent a minute apart that first month. But now he seems to look for reasons to be away from me, and we seem to fight all the time. I don't treat *him* any differently, but he sure doesn't treat *me* the way he used to. I don't understand it."

Lisa had been married once before, to Christopher, and the story was similar. They had fallen in love immediately, and within six months they were married and certain they would be ecstatically happy for the rest of their lives. But in the first year of their marriage, there were already signs that the magic of their relationship was escaping them. They began to find fault with each other over little things. Roses and kisses gradually gave way to expectations and disappointments, each of which left a wound and then a scar. Slowly, the excitement of being in love became a distant memory. Unable to find the happiness they sought, they divorced after eight years of marriage.

Lisa had tried very hard to make her relationship with Christopher work. She'd tried sacrifice, pleading, complaining, compromise, self-help books, professional counseling, and visits to her minister, but nothing she did seemed to help. And because she didn't see *why* her relationship had failed, she was doomed to repeat her mistakes with Doug and to continue being unhappy. We can all benefit from understanding Lisa's experience, because it's typical of the pattern seen in virtually every unhappy relationship—not only between spouses, but also between friends, family members, people in the workplace, and so on. We've all had the experience of starting a relationship that seemed promising, only to have something go wrong that we didn't understand, and when that happened, we were left feeling disappointed or worse. We must understand what happens in these situations, or we'll repeat the process again and again.

When we're unhappy, it seems natural for us to blame a partner—a spouse, a friend, a child, even a relative stranger—for our feelings, mainly because that's what everyone else does. All our lives we've heard variations of statements like "You make me so mad," or "He makes me so angry," until we've come to believe that other people have the power to determine how *we* feel. Because other people have often pointed out how *their* anger was caused by our mistakes, we have learned to justify *our* anger by pointing out the mistakes of others. And because people are always making mistakes, it's easy to find justification for our blaming and anger.

Sadly, it's a common pattern: If we become unhappy in our relationships, we turn our partners into scapegoats for everything we don't like, and we blame them for all the unhappiness in our lives, including the unhappiness we carried with us for the many years before we even met them. But we are mistaken to blame our partners for our negative feelings. It's just the excuse we use because we feel bad, we don't know why, and we need someone other than ourselves to blame. Until we understand that, we cannot learn to have truly loving and lasting relationships.

The Missing Ingredient

Imagine that after a violent storm, you and I are shipwrecked on a barren island in the middle of the ocean. After a week with nothing to eat, I begin to complain that you're not doing enough to provide food for me, and the hungrier I become, the more I complain. Not an hour goes by that I don't remind you that I'm starving and you are to blame.

You must think I'm insane. Obviously you didn't cause my hunger. I'm starving because a storm wrecked our ship and left us stranded on an island without food—and you had nothing to do with any of that. My blaming you is not only wrong, it's ineffective, because it does nothing to help solve our predicament. Two starving people with no source of food cannot possibly give each other what they need, and no amount of anger or blame can change that.

And so it is with relationships. When we're unhappy, our misery is not the fault of our partner. Blaming that person is therefore foolish, wasteful, and destructive, because no matter how much we demand or insist, he or she cannot *make* us happy. We're unhappy because we're starving for the one ingredient that's most essential to genuine happiness, and it was missing long before we met our partner.

That ingredient—the one thing that creates happiness and fulfilling relationships—is *Real Love,* unconditional love. It's that simple. When we learn what Real Love is, and when we find it, our unhappiness disappears just as surely as hunger vanishes in the presence of food. Loving relationships then become natural and effortless. But most of us have not experienced Real Love. As a result, we're emotionally and spiritually starving and are unable to make each other happy, no matter how hard we try.

Real Love and Genuine Happiness

Real Love is caring about the happiness of another person without any thought for what we might get for ourselves. When we give Real Love, we're not disappointed, hurt, or angry, even when people are thoughtless or inconsiderate or give us nothing in return—including gratitude—because our concern is for *their* happiness, not our own. Real Love is unconditional.

It's Real Love when other people care about *our* happiness without any concern for themselves. They're not disappointed or angry when we make our foolish mistakes, when we don't do what they want, or even when we inconvenience them personally.

> Real Love is unconditionally caring about the happiness of another person.

Sadly, few of us have either given or received that kind of love, and without it we experience a terrible void in our lives, which we try to fill with money, power, food, approval, sex, and entertainment. But no matter how much of those substitutes we acquire, we remain empty, alone, afraid, and angry, because the one thing we *really* need is Real Love. Without it, we can only be miserable; with it, our happiness is guaranteed.

When I use the word *happiness,* I do not mean the fleeting pleasure we get from money, sex, and conditional approval. Nor do I mean the brief feeling of relief we experience during the temporary absence of conflict or disaster. Real happiness is not the feeling we get from being entertained or making people do what we want. Genuine happiness is a profound and lasting sense of peace and fulfillment that deeply satisfies and enlarges the soul. It doesn't go away when circumstances get difficult. It survives and even grows through hardship and struggle. True happiness is our entire reason to live, and that kind of happiness can only be obtained as we find Real Love and share it with others. *With Real Love, nothing else matters; without it, nothing else is enough.*

The greatest fear of all for a human being is to be unloved and alone. As a physician, I saw that confirmed many times by people who knew they were dying. Those people were consistently more afraid that no one cared about them and that they would die *alone* than they were of death itself. We all have a deep yearning to feel connected to each other, and when that connection is missing, we are terrified.

When someone is genuinely concerned about our happiness, we do feel that connection to another person. We feel included in his or her life, and in that instant we are *no longer alone.* Each moment of unconditional acceptance creates a living thread to the person who accepts us, and these threads weave a powerful bond that fills us with a genuine and lasting happiness. Nothing but Real Love can do that. In addition, when we know that even one person loves us unconditionally, we feel a connection to everyone else. We feel included in the family of all mankind, of which that one person is a part.

Because so few of us have ever experienced unconditional love in our lives, and because the effect is so powerful, I want to give you a small taste of it. I encourage you to slow down right now and really take your time as you read the next four paragraphs. If possible, read them in a room by yourself and take the time to contemplate them deeply as you open your mind to the possibilities they suggest.

Picture yourself relaxing in the back of a chauffeur-driven car. You're on the way to a town two hours away. It's a small town you've never visited. In fact, no one knows about this place but you and the people who live there. Although it's a beautiful place situated in a lovely valley, you're not going there to see the sights. You're going because everyone there is genuinely happy. They're happy because they all feel loved. In this place there is no fear or anger. And you're going because they've invited you.

As you pull up to the house where you'll stay, dozens of people surround your car, touch you gently, help you into the house, ask about your trip, and look at you in a way you've never seen or felt before. You sense with absolute certainty that the only concern of everyone in that town is *your* happiness. Because they have everything that really matters in life—because they feel loved and happy themselves—they don't need you to do anything for them, and you know that. So you know there is nothing you can do to disappoint them or hurt them.

As you communicate with these new friends, you can see that it doesn't matter to them whether you're smart or pretty or handsome. You don't have to do anything to impress them or get them to like you. They truly don't care if you say something stupid or if you make mistakes. It finally and powerfully occurs to you that it's impossible to be embarrassed or ashamed around these people—because they love you no matter what you do.

That is the feeling of being unconditionally loved—and many of us simply can't imagine it, even as a mental exercise. We've been judged, criticized, and conditionally supported for so long that the idea of being unconditionally accepted is inconceivable. But I have seen what happens when people consistently take the steps that lead to finding Real Love, which I'll be discussing in the following chapters. For now I simply want to assure you that you, too, can find this kind of happiness and that it will utterly transform your life. I ask you to temporarily put your doubts on the shelf and allow for the possibility that Real Love exists, and that you can find it. I make that suggestion because in an atmosphere of skepticism and fear, you cannot experience Real Love, even when it's offered.

Feeling loved and becoming unconditionally loving doesn't happen all at once. You won't lose your fear, pain, disappointment, and anger overnight. Experiencing Real Love takes time and patience, and you'll stumble and fall along the way, as I do every day. But the journey is well worth every effort. This is not a fantasy. Thousands of people have successfully used this simple process to find Real Love, genuine happiness, and fulfilling relationships.

> With Real Love, nothing else matters; without it, nothing else is enough.

At this point, you may be thinking, *But we can't just unconditionally love people when they're wrong. Somebody has to speak up when mistakes are made.* And it's true that we sometimes do have the responsibility to teach and correct people—children and employees, for example. But that never has to be done with disappointment and anger, the two signs that always reveal that our true motivation is to get something for ourselves—and that is not Real Love.

You might also be worried that loving unconditionally would turn you into a doormat, to be used by everyone around you. But loving people unconditionally does not mean you have the responsibility to give them everything they want. That would just be indulgent and irresponsible. When we love people unconditionally, we accept them as they are and contribute to their happiness as wisely as we can. That does not imply that we respond to their every demand.

The Destructive Legacy of Conditional Love

Real Love is "I care how **you** feel." Conditional love is "I like how you make **me** feel." Conditional love is what people give to us when we do what they want, and it's the only kind of love that most of us have ever known. People have liked us more when we made them feel good, or at least when we did nothing to inconvenience them. In other words, we have to *buy* conditional love from the people around us.

It's critical that we be able to distinguish between Real Love and conditional love. When we can't do that, we tend to settle for giving and receiving conditional love, which leaves us empty, unhappy, and frustrated. Fortunately, there are two reliable signs that love is not genuine: **disappointment** and **anger**. Every time we frown, sigh with disappointment, speak harshly, or in any way express our anger at other people, we're communicating that we're not getting what **we** want. At least in that moment, we are not caring for our partner's happiness, but only for our own. Our partner then senses our selfishness and feels disconnected from us and alone, no matter what we say or do.

> If you're feeling disappointed or angry with your partner, it's a sure sign you're not unconditionally loving him or her.

Most of us have received little, if any, Real Love. We prove that every day with the evidence of our unhappiness—our fear, anger, blaming, withdrawal, manipulation, controlling, and so on. People who know they're unconditionally loved don't feel and do those things. But most of us have been taught since childhood to do without Real Love and to settle instead for giving and receiving conditional love. Let me use myself as an example. As a child, I was thrilled when my mother smiled at me, spoke softly, and held me, because I knew from those behaviors that she loved me. I also noticed that she did those pleasant things more often when I was "good"—when I was quiet, grateful, and cooperative. In other words, I saw that she loved me more when I did what she liked, something almost all parents understandably do.

When I was "bad"—noisy, disobedient, and otherwise inconvenient—she did not speak softly or smile at me. On those occasions, she frowned, sighed with disappointment, and often spoke in a harsh tone of voice. *Although it was certainly unintentional,* she clearly told me with those behaviors that she loved me less, and that was the worst pain in the world for me.

Giving or withholding acceptance based on another person's

behavior is the essence of conditional love, and nearly all of us were loved that way as children. When we made the football team, got good grades, and washed the dishes without being asked, our parents naturally looked happy and said things like "Way to go!" or "I'm so proud of you." But when we failed a class at school, or tracked mud across the carpet, or fought with our siblings, or wrecked the car, did our parents smile at us then? Did they pat us on the shoulder and speak kindly as they corrected us? No, with rare exceptions they did not. Without thinking, they frowned, rolled their eyes, and sighed with exasperation. They used a tone of voice that was *not* the one we heard when we did what they wanted and made them look good. Some of us were even yelled at or physically abused when we were "bad."

Other people in our childhood also gave us conditional approval. Schoolteachers smiled and encouraged us when we were bright and cooperative, but they behaved quite differently when we were slow and difficult. Even our own friends liked us more when we did what they liked. In fact, that's what made them our friends. And that pattern of conditional approval has continued throughout our lives. People continue to give us their approval more often when we do what they want. And so we do what it takes to earn it.

Although it is given unintentionally, conditional acceptance has an unspeakably disastrous effect, because it fails to form the bonds of human connection created by Real Love. As a result, no matter how much conditional love we receive, we still feel empty, alone, and miserable. And although we like to believe otherwise, because we have received conditional love from others all our lives, that's what we tend to give to those around us. We naturally pass on what we were given.

We like to believe we're unconditionally loving, but in

most cases we're not. We prove that each time we're disappointed or irritated with another person. We like to think we unconditionally love our spouse or children, but then we become annoyed when they don't do what we want, or when they're not grateful for the things we do for them. As we've discussed, the origin of our irritation is not what they've done (or not done), but the lack of Real Love in our own lives. Fortunately, you can now learn how to make decisions that will bring more Real Love and genuine happiness into your life.

If you're unhappy, don't look to your partner for the cause. You're unhappy because you don't feel unconditionally loved yourself and because you're not sufficiently unconditionally loving toward others. Both conditions have existed for a long time, usually from early childhood. Because your parents are responsible for the love you received as a child, and because any child who does not receive sufficient Real Love is necessarily filled with emptiness and fear, your parents are certainly responsible, to a large extent, for the way you feel and function as an adult. But you need to understand that as an adult you have become increasingly responsible for your own happiness. And so, exactly how much can you hold your parents accountable for your present condition? That would be impossible to quantify. But no matter what the exact extent of your parents' responsibility, it is definitely not *productive* to blame them for your present unhappiness—while it *is* useful to *understand* their role in your life. *Understanding* is a simple, realistic assessment of how things are, but *blame* implies anger, which can only be harmful to both yourself and others.

I've never met a parent who got up in the morning and thought, *Today I could unconditionally love and teach my children and fill their lives with joy. But, no, I think I'll be selfish, critical, and demanding instead.* You need to understand that your parents loved you as well as they knew how and that they certainly didn't set out to cause you emotional pain. The fact is that if they themselves didn't have enough experience with Real Love, they couldn't possibly have given you the Real Love you required. Moreover, *you* are now responsible for the decisions that will make you loving and happy, and if you continue to be resentful and angry, you will not make wise decisions in the present.

> Don't blame your partner for your unhappiness, which is really caused by a long-standing lack of Real Love in your life.

When I talk to people about their unhappy lives and relationships, I don't dwell on the past. I don't make them victims of their past experiences. However, I find that it is occasionally useful to make them aware of what effect their past has had on their present unhappiness. Cheryl was very unhappy, and she blamed it all on her husband. I explained to her that her husband was not the cause of her unhappiness. "Your life was incomplete long before you met your husband," I told her. "You came to your marriage already missing something, and you hoped your husband would supply what was missing and make you happy. When he didn't do that, you blamed him for not fixing everything in your life. You were missing the one thing in life that we all must have in order to be happy and to have loving relationships."

"And what's that?" asked Cheryl.

"Real Love—unconditional love. When people don't get enough unconditional love as children, they feel terribly empty and afraid. People who feel empty and afraid can't be happy, and they can't have loving relationships, because they're too busy filling their own needs and protecting themselves. You hoped your husband would love you unconditionally, but he couldn't because he'd never been unconditionally loved himself. He, in turn, hoped you would unconditionally love *him,* but you couldn't, either, because you hadn't been unconditionally loved in *your* childhood. Neither of you had the love that's required to make a successful relationship. So you tried to make each other happy with other things: praise, sex, money, control, things like that. But those things never last for long."

"But I did feel loved. My parents *did* love me," Cheryl insisted.

I've heard many people say that, and they're always sincere. Who, after all, wants to believe his own parents didn't love him? "How often," I asked her, "did your father hold you and tell you he loved you? How many times each day was he obviously delighted when you entered the room? How often did your mother sit with you and ask what was happening in your life—just to listen, not to give advice?"

Cheryl was speechless. Although she'd been raised by parents who were as good as any she knew, she couldn't think of a single time when any of those things had happened.

I continued. "What happened when you made mistakes and disappointed your parents? Did you feel just as loved then as when you were 'good'?"

As Cheryl described the details of her childhood, it became obvious that her father had mostly avoided her. Her mother had been kind when Cheryl was obedient, but she was critical and harsh when Cheryl "misbehaved." Finally, Cheryl realized that she had never felt unconditionally loved. I then made it clear that there was no blaming in this, just an attempt to understand the real cause of the fear and anger in her life.

Once Cheryl understood that her emptiness, fear, and

anger had been caused by a lifetime of feeling unloved, two very important things happened: First, she experienced a dramatic change in attitude toward her husband. She stopped blaming him for her unhappiness. That blame alone had nearly destroyed their marriage. Second, she began to take the steps necessary to find the Real Love she needed, and that changed her life completely. We often need to see that we were not unconditionally loved in the past, not so we can blame our parents or any particular person, but so we can *stop* blaming the partners we have now and begin to find the Real Love we need to create the genuine happiness we all want.

Some of you may believe that if our childhood was less than perfect, we just need to "get over it," like a bad dream. You may think that what we were given (or not given) so long ago couldn't possibly continue to affect us now. But look what happened to Cheryl because she'd failed to receive Real Love as a child. Without the most important ingredient for happiness, she grew up empty and afraid. As I spoke with her further, I learned that she'd reacted to her emptiness and fear by manipulating and controlling all of the people around her, not just her husband. She was destroying her life, and without Real Love that's what people continue to do, all the way into their seventies and eighties.

You can't build a solid house on a rotten, shifting foundation. But if you were not unconditionally loved as a child, that's the kind of foundation you have, and no effort you put into the walls, windows, and doors will ever be fulfilling. You have to fix the foundation. Fortunately, as you find Real Love now, you can heal all the wounds of the past, repair the foundation, and build the kind of life you've always wanted.

Drowning for Lack of Love

Imagine yourself again in the middle of the ocean, but this time there's no boat, no island, and no one to help you. You're drowning out there all by yourself. You're exhausted and terrified. Suddenly, a man grabs you from behind and drags you under the water. Completely overwhelmed by fear and anger, you struggle wildly to get free, but no matter what you do, your head remains underwater.

Just as you're about to pass out and drown, I arrive in a small boat and pull you from the water. After catching your breath, you turn and see that the man who dragged you under is actually drowning himself and only grabbed you in a desperate attempt to save his own life. He wasn't trying to harm you at all. Once you realize that, your anger vanishes immediately and you quickly help him into the boat.

That's how it is with relationships. People really don't do things with the principal goal of hurting *you*. When people hurt you, they're like the man who dragged you under the water—they're simply drowning and trying to save *themselves*. People who don't feel unconditionally loved are desperate and will do almost anything to eliminate the pain of their emptiness. Unfortunately, as they struggle to get the things that give them temporary relief—approval, money, sex, power, and so on—their behavior often has a negative effect on the people around them, including you. But that is not their first intent. Other people hurt us only because they're reacting badly to the pain of feeling unloved and alone. When we truly understand that, our feelings toward people, and our relationships with them, will change dramatically.

Without Real Love, we feel like we're drowning all the time. In that condition, almost everything seems threatening to us, even the most innocent behaviors. When people get

angry or criticize us, we don't see them as drowning and protecting themselves. We become afraid, defensive, and angry,
and we respond by using behaviors that may hurt *them*. Naturally, they react by protecting themselves and hurting us
with even greater intensity, and until we understand that Real
Love is the solution, we can only perpetuate this cycle of self-
protection and injury.

Most relationships fail because we become angry and
blame our anger on something our partner did or did not do.
We need to remember that our anger is actually a reaction to
the feelings of helplessness and fear that result from a lifetime
of struggling to survive without unconditional love. Getting
angry and assigning blame may give us a fleeting sense of
power that momentarily relieves our fear, but those feelings
originate within us, not with our partner's behavior.

When the man dragged you under the water, he did not
cause your angry reaction. Your anger was the result of a series
of many events that led to your drowning in the ocean, and
also a result of your own decision to blame that man for
drowning you. You weren't murderously angry with the man
in the water because of a single tug on your shoulder. You
were angry because you'd been spit out in the middle of the
ocean with no chance for survival and because you were exhausted and frightened and about to die. What the other
man did just added the last straw to the camel's back and *appeared* to be the cause of your anger.

Similarly, the anger we feel toward our partners results
from past events (whether or not we felt Real Love—mostly
from our parents) and present decisions (whether we choose
to be angry or loving with our partners). We're reacting to a
lifetime of trying to survive without unconditional love, and
anger is an understandable response because it makes us feel
less helpless and afraid—for the moment. It protects us and

briefly makes us feel better. But it never makes us feel loved or happy or less alone.

We need to learn a better response to our pain than blaming and anger, and we can. As we come to understand that our partners are not to blame for our unhappiness, we can better exercise self-control to curb our anger. Then, as we begin to find and experience Real Love, we'll feel as if we're being pulled out of the water and into the boat. In the absence of the terrible fear that accompanies drowning, we'll no longer have a *need* to protect ourselves with anger—or any of the other unproductive behaviors we use in relationships, such as lying, acting hurt, and withdrawing. Our ability to form and maintain loving relationships will then come simply and easily.

Just as being pulled into the boat instantly allowed you to gain the correct perspective on the man who was drowning you, understanding Real Love will provide you with the ability to discern the difference between the "right" and "wrong" decisions you make in your life and in your relationships. First, I suggest that being genuinely happy is the ultimate goal in life and is therefore also the ultimate good. Second, because Real Love is absolutely essential to our happiness, I suggest that anything that interferes with our ability to feel and share unconditional love is necessarily "bad" or "wrong," while anything that promotes our ability to feel loved and share that love with others is "right" and "good."

2

Getting and Protecting

The Many Faces of Imitation Love

Without Real Love, our emptiness is intolerably painful. We're starving to death, and we'll do anything to eliminate our discomfort—even if the relief we obtain is quite temporary and the overall effect of our behavior is destructive to ourselves and to others. We attempt to fill our emptiness with whatever feels good in the moment. We use money, the conditional "love" of others, anger, sex, alcohol, drugs, violence, and so on, all of which are variations of only four general things: *praise, power, pleasure,* and *safety.* When we pursue these things as substitutes for Real Love, they all become forms of Imitation Love.

The Many Faces of Imitation Love

Praise comes in many varieties—flattery, gratitude, approval, respect, sex, and money, among others—and we love them all. When people tell us how wonderful we are, we temporarily believe we're worthwhile. In the absence of Real Love, we

18

convince ourselves that flattery is genuine affection instead of seeing it for what it really is: praise we have to earn. We spend countless hours and dollars on makeup, hairstyling, clothing, exercise, even plastic surgery, all in the hope of *earning* the words "You look great." We work hard at school, in our jobs, and at home just so people will compliment our intelligence, creativity, and diligence. Our obsession with winning—in sports, business, and even everyday arguments—is also motivated by a desire to be flattered.

We tend to judge each other by our financial success, and we prove that with our endless curiosity about each other's jobs, incomes, investments, houses, cars, and boats. Even in conversations with relative strangers, we're almost always asked, "What do you do for a living?" If we say we're the chief executive officer of a *Fortune* 500 corporation, our companions tend to judge us worthy of further conversation, but their reaction is considerably less enthusiastic if we say we're a street sweeper. We hope that money and success will make us deserving of approval, which we then wishfully interpret as a kind of affection. It's only Imitation Love, but in the absence of Real Love, it feels pretty good, and many of us are quite willing to devote our entire lives to the pursuit of it.

When we don't feel unconditionally loved, our need for praise is unbounded, and much of that need is filled—however briefly—when other people find us sexually desirable. Most young men and women—and older ones, too—want to look like the models on the covers of magazines. We spend long hours worrying, scheming, and manipulating others so they will respect our strength, capability, and financial success—and all because we so badly want people to think well of us.

We love it when people say thank-you to us, because we take it as a form of praise for our performance. It makes us feel important and worthwhile. In fact, we often do things for people just so we can receive their gratitude. We prove that every time we're disappointed and even angry on the occasions when we *don't* receive an expression of appreciation for something we've done for someone else. But people who feel unconditionally loving don't require gratitude for the things they do. Their concern is for the happiness of other people.

In the absence of Real Love, we enjoy the sensation of **power** we get from manipulating other people. We use money, authority, sex, flattery, and personal persuasion to influence, control, and even hurt people. We actually feel some sense of connection to the people we control. The bond is shallow and fleeting, but it feels better than the pain of being completely alone, and it gives us a momentary sense of emotional excitement.

If we're in a position of authority—in business, politics, the family, or in any organization—we can often make people do what we want, which makes us feel powerful, and then we feel less of the terrible helplessness that always accompanies the lack of unconditional love in our lives. As people follow our direction, we can also persuade ourselves that somehow they approve of us, which is something we want badly.

Money has always been a great source of power. We can really make things happen with money, and we like that. Money makes trucks move, planes take off, and people scurry to satisfy our desires. It can even buy temporary friends and sex. But it can't buy unconditional love, the only thing that will make us truly happy.

Imagine a young girl who gets little or no respect from her parents, teachers, or even her peers. She feels alone and helpless. But if she becomes sexually attractive, she quickly discovers that she can use her appearance and sexual behavior to influence and even control the thoughts and behavior of boys and men in a powerful way. It's an exciting and seductive experience. In the absence of Real Love, she's getting a lot of Imitation Love in the form of power.

The pursuit of **pleasure** is a way to distract ourselves from the emptiness and pain that always accompany a lack of Real Love. One of the most common ways we look for pleasure is through sexual gratification. To get an idea of the degree to which our society is obsessed with sexual pleasure, we need only make a brief scrutiny of our movies, magazines, television shows, and the Internet. Or we might pursue pleasure in the excitement of watching sports, watching television, traveling, even eating. All of these pursuits can be healthy and fulfilling, unless we're using them as a substitute for the infinitely more fulfilling happiness of Real Love or as a way to avoid facing our personal emptiness and our inability to find and maintain loving relationships. And if our pain becomes too great, we may try to distract ourselves in any number of progressively destructive ways, ranging from playing too many video games and watching too many violent movies to drinking too much alcohol and taking mind-altering drugs.

Without Real Love, we're already in the worst kind of pain, and we'll go to great lengths to keep ourselves **safe** from experiencing more pain. If we can't have genuine acceptance, we can at least do everything in our power to avoid more disapproval. One way to minimize the risk of criticism and pain is to avoid doing anything unfamiliar. So we stay in the same boring, dead-end jobs, attempt to learn nothing new, and continue in stagnant, unrewarding—but predictable—relationships. When we're not being actively injured by something or someone, we confuse that safety with real happiness.

>   In the absence of Real Love, we attempt to fill our emptiness with Imitation Love, which comes in four forms: praise, power, pleasure, and safety.

The Cost of Imitation Love

We love it when people say nice things to us. But we've all learned from considerable experience that most people praise us only when we're doing what they like. We then have to <u>work hard to keep pleasing them and earning their approval.</u> <u>We're trapped.</u> Earning praise becomes a never-ending burden, costing us far more than we get from it. And that's true with every form of Imitation Love.

In addition, no matter how much excitement or reward we get from the pursuit of Imitation Love in the beginning, the excitement always wears off. Remember how thrilling it was the first time you were paid a dollar for doing some chore? You got a feeling of praise from that dollar, and maybe a little power. But that feeling wore off quickly. And it wasn't long before it took a lot more than a dollar to give you the same thrill. Imitation Love is very much like an addictive drug. The effect wears off quickly, and over time we need more and more of it to get the same brief effect.

But we still haven't talked about the most dangerous cost of Imitation Love, which is that no matter how much of it we acquire, we never get the feeling of connection with other people that comes with Real Love, so we're still fatally alone. Unfortunately, Imitation Love *does feel good*—it does feel better than nothing at all—and if we can convince ourselves that we feel "good enough," we just might waste our entire lives pursuing this false sense of happiness instead of finding the Real Love and genuine happiness that are available to us. In the absence of Real Love, we often allow ourselves to believe that we're actually loved and happy when we get enough Imitation Love. An ocean of Imitation Love lacks the power to create the happiness found in a teaspoon of the real thing, but if we don't know about Real Love, we'll gladly fall for the deception of the imitation. That is the ultimate tragedy of life.

I'm not saying, however, that praise, power, pleasure, and safety are always bad. They're dangerous only when they're used as substitutes for Real Love and genuine happiness. When two people really care about each other's happiness, *praise* becomes nourishing and fun, not contrived and manipulative. Under those conditions, each partner experiences the real *power* that comes from being loving and happy. Both partners feel the genuine *safety* that comes from being cared for by one another. And sex—as one of many examples of *pleasure*—becomes healthy and delightful, because it's a natural expression of Real Love instead of a substitute for it.

If Imitation Love leaves us feeling empty and miserable, why do we keep pursuing it? Because living without unconditional love and feeling alone are unbearable, and we'll do almost *anything* to get rid of those feelings, however superficial and temporary the relief might be.

Chuck was fifteen years old. His mother told him every day—often without saying a word—that he was messy and a huge inconvenience to her. His father told him he was clumsy and irresponsible. Understandably, Chuck felt unimportant, unloved, empty, and alone. And then he discovered that Melanie, a fourteen-year-old girl down the street, thought he was cute and smart and actually enjoyed his company. Wow! Suddenly he felt important and powerful. He also enjoyed the excitement of physically touching her and eventually having sex with her. All this Imitation Love was the best thing he'd ever known, and he clung to it like a drowning man.

When Chuck's parents learned he was having sex with Melanie, they angrily forbade him to see her again. But, not surprisingly, he ignored them and continued to see her. He was not about to let go of the only thing he'd found that had ever relieved the intolerable emptiness and pain he'd felt all his life. That reasoning didn't justify his behavior, but it certainly explained it.

> Although the effects are superficial and temporary, we still pursue Imitation Love in its many forms, because it gives us a sense of "happiness" that feels far better than nothing in the absence of Real Love.

Getting and Protecting Behaviors

The absence of unconditional love creates an emptiness we cannot ignore. Because of that, our subsequent behavior is often completely determined by our *need* to be loved and our *fear* of not being loved. Without Real Love, we do whatever it takes—Getting Behaviors—to fill our sense of emptiness with Imitation Love. And we also use Protecting Behaviors to eliminate our fear. The Getting Behaviors include lying, attacking, acting like a victim, and running. The Protecting Behaviors include lying, attacking, acting like a victim, and clinging.

We've learned from countless experiences that when we inconvenience people with our mistakes, they tend to express their disappointment and anger toward us. We then feel less loved and more alone, the feelings that terrify us the most. To keep that from happening, we lie about our mistakes. We hide who we really are.

If you watch two people in conversation, you'll see that each of them is carefully and unconsciously studying the other for any hint of disapproval—a forehead wrinkling into a frown, an eyebrow lifting into an expression of doubt, a corner of the mouth turning down, a change in tone of voice—and when that happens, the speaker immediately modifies what he or she is saying until all those signs of disapproval disappear. In most cases we don't even know we're doing this. However, that modification of what we say and do to please other people is **lying**—because we don't tell our partners that we're trying to get them to like us (lying as a Getting Behavior) and protect ourselves from their disapproval (lying as a Protecting Behavior).

We lie in other ways as well. When we tell people about our accomplishments but not our flaws, hide our true feelings, change our physical appearance to attract people to us, or tell people what we know they want to hear so they'll like us—we're lying. We're lying when we fail to take complete responsibility for what we do, when we tell only the partial truth about our mistakes, and when we shift the blame to as many other people as we can. We're also lying when we don't take responsibility for our own feelings, such as when we blame other people for "making" us angry. With our lies, we get Imitation Love in the form of praise, power, pleasure, and safety. We do this so often—and so unconsciously—we think it's normal.

***

Attacking is any behavior that motivates another person through *fear* to behave in a way we want. For example, with anger—probably the most common form of attacking—we can make most people sufficiently uncomfortable (afraid) that they'll do whatever we want in order to stop us from making them feel bad. With our anger, we can get people to give us attention, respect, power, flattery, approval, even sex. But of course, if they're giving us these things not because they're genuinely concerned for our happiness, but simply to avoid our anger, all we're receiving is Imitation Love. We're using anger as a Getting Behavior—to win arguments, impress people, and make ourselves feel strong—and as a Protecting Behavior to prevent other people from hurting or threatening us and to keep ourselves safe.

In addition to anger, we attack by making people feel guilty, criticizing them, withdrawing approval, physically intimidating them, and using our positions of authority at work, at home, and elsewhere, all in order to get Imitation Love and to protect ourselves from fear.

If we can convince people that we've been injured and treated unfairly, they'll often stop hurting us and give us their sympathy, attention, and support. That's why we **act like victims.** Victims are always saying variations on the following three sentences: (1) Look what you did *to* me. (2) Look what you should have done *for* me (and didn't). (3) It's not my fault. Victims have excuses for everything and blame everyone but themselves for their own mistakes and unhappiness. We've all acted like a victim at some time in our life. Whenever we're confronted with a mistake we've made and say, "I couldn't help it," we're acting like a victim.

If we simply move away from a source of pain, we're less likely to be hurt. Withdrawing, avoiding people, leaving relationships, and being shy are all forms of **running**. Drugs and alcohol are other ways to run.

***

Clinging is obvious when a child grips tightly to his mother's skirt. But we also cling emotionally to those people who give us attention, hoping we can sometimes squeeze even more out of them. We may do this by flattering the people who do things for us, or by being excessively grateful. We can sometimes cling by telling people how much we love them and need them. Another way to cling is by giving gifts that we hope will obligate others to feel affection for us. These are all forms of manipulation that we use—usually unconsciously—to get more of what we want from people. Effectively, we're begging for more Imitation Love.

> We use Getting Behaviors to fill our emptiness: lying, attacking, acting like a victim, and clinging. We use Protecting Behaviors to eliminate our fear: lying, attacking, acting like a victim, and running.

Getting and Protecting—Why Do We Do That?

At heart, we all know that lying, attacking other people, acting like victims, running, and clinging are not responsible and "right" behaviors. In fact, when confronted about these behaviors, we usually hide them. So why do we use them? Because we get a lot from them. In the absence of Real Love, these behaviors protect us from pain and fill our emptiness, and they usually produce an immediate response. When I get angry, for example, I can often get people to do what I want much more quickly than if I use gentle persuasion. That's a real inducement to use anger. As a child, I learned that it was faster and less painful to lie about breaking the window than to confess, listen to a long lecture, experience the horror of my parents' affection withdrawing, clean up the mess, pay for the window, listen to another lecture when the window was replaced, and hold my breath waiting for more lectures each time I hit a baseball around the house. Is it any wonder that children grow up to lie as adults? The rewards of using Getting and Protecting Behaviors are great.

But the costs of using those behaviors are much greater. Lying, being angry, and manipulating people for attention take a lot of work. And after all that effort, the satisfaction is gone in an instant. The effects of Imitation Love are brief, and then we have to start earning it all over again. Still, most of us devote our entire lives to these hopelessly unfulfilling activities. And in the end, we never get the deep connection of Real Love we need and want.

In addition, the Getting and Protecting Behaviors drive people away from us and bankrupt the very relationships we want to enrich. We use them for short-term gain, but we cause enormous long-term damage. For example, you may use anger to win an argument with a partner, but can you remember the last time your anger made you feel more unconditionally loved by someone, or more loving toward him? You may get out of trouble by lying to someone, but you'll never deeply enrich your relationship by doing that. When we do things to get Imitation Love and to protect ourselves, our partners sense that and pull away from us emotionally.

The worst effect of Getting and Protecting Behaviors, however, is that *they make it impossible for us to feel Real Love,* even when it's actually being given to us. Whenever we manipulate people in any way for something we want, we know that what we receive is purchased, not freely offered. We're paying for what we get, whether we needed to or not. We'll be discussing why that is in the following chapter. For the moment, you just need to understand that when we use Getting and Protecting Behaviors, we exhaust ourselves, we spend our lives for nothing, we guarantee that we'll never feel loved, and we hurt the people around us.

If that's true, if Getting and Protecting Behaviors are so terrible, why don't we stop using them? Because we're rarely conscious of them. A drowning man doesn't mean to hurt other people; in his state of mindless panic, he simply can't seem to stop himself from grabbing anything or anyone that might help to keep his head above the water. His fear is so overwhelming that he doesn't think for a second about the harm he might cause others as he saves himself.

Without Real Love, our fear of being unloved and alone is overwhelming. We then use our Getting and Protecting Behaviors in a state of panic very similar to that of a drowning man. Our primary intent is not to hurt other people or do anything wrong; our real goal is only to eliminate our own emptiness, fear, and pain. When we really understand that, the way we see our own behavior and the behavior of others will change forever. We will no longer feel excessively guilty for our own behavior, nor will we be angry at others for using those same behaviors.

All our lives we've been taught that when we inconvenience and hurt other people, we're "bad," morally defective, even monstrous. We're supposed to feel guilty when we offend another person. And we all feel entirely justified in being angry at those evil people who dare to violate all that is right and good by inconveniencing and hurting *us.* Our society virtually revolves around the principles of guilt and anger.

The guilty must pay. If we are the guilty ones, we must feel great remorse and wallow in our guilt. If others have transgressed, then we feel justified in venting our anger against them.

But all that guilt and anger turn to dust when we understand our need for Real Love and the reasons for our natural use of Getting and Protecting Behaviors when we don't have it. When we lie, attack people, act like victims, and run, it's not because we're bad or wish to hurt other people. We do those things because we're empty and afraid, and we hope they will protect us and fill our lives with Imitation Love. Those are the only behaviors we know—the ones we learned from our childhood. That does *not* justify our behavior, but it certainly explains it.

It's a huge waste of time, energy, and happiness to wallow in excessive guilt when we make mistakes. How much more productive it is to simply *see* our mistakes clearly and learn from them. In most cases, the problem is a lack of Real Love, which we can solve by taking the simple steps we'll describe in Chapter Four. In addition, we need to exercise our own self-control in changing our behavior, something we'll talk about in several subsequent chapters.

Similarly, when other people make mistakes—even when they inconvenience and hurt *us*—we need to remember that they, too, are simply empty and afraid. Seeing the mistakes of others in this way doesn't change the fact that their behavior may be selfish or counterproductive, but it does make it possible for us not to be angry and to give them what they really need—someone to understand and help them. They don't need yet another person to be angry at them and punish them, which only adds to their pain and actually increases the likelihood that they'll use even more Getting and Protecting

Behaviors. Anger and punishment do not make people happier. That doesn't mean, however, that there's no place for negative consequences, even prisons, when people keep making poor decisions—but we'll be discussing the subject of consequences in a later chapter.

———

Matthew's life provides a prime example of Getting and Protecting Behaviors. Although he had a great job, plenty of money, a beautiful wife, and all the things most people work all their lives to achieve, Matthew was not happy. He tried therapy, self-help books, and going to church, but nothing worked—he was still discouraged and depressed.

There had been nothing obviously unusual about Matthew's childhood. His parents weren't divorced, and they didn't yell at him or beat him. But they did what almost all parents do: When Matthew was a "good" boy, they smiled and spoke kindly to him; when he was noisy, messy, and inconvenient, they frowned, spoke harshly, and withdrew their affection. Without Real Love, Matthew could only feel empty and afraid, so he responded with Getting Behaviors to fill his emptiness with Imitation Love, and Protecting Behaviors to eliminate his fears.

As a small boy, Matthew learned to lie when he made mistakes. When he did that, he avoided the disapproval of his parents and others. When lying didn't work, he acted like a victim to get sympathy. He studied diligently in school to get good grades and win the approval of his parents and teachers. He learned to use anger to get what he wanted from his siblings and his peers. He was a master of Getting and Protecting Behaviors by the time he left grade school. He didn't consciously realize he was trying to earn or buy affection, but he was still living a lie in order to gain the praise, power, pleasure, and safety that would make him feel good. And because he was doing what everyone around him was doing, it all seemed quite normal.

As an adult, he continued the same behaviors that had served him as a child: He worked hard to advance his career in order to buy the respect of his family and peers. When he made mistakes, he covered them up or blamed them on others. He used his positions of authority, at work and at home, to intimidate people so they wouldn't confront him about his mistakes. And when he felt sufficiently threatened by a relationship, he simply withdrew.

Matthew was just reacting to his desperate need for Real Love and his fear that no one would ever love him. But with all his Getting and Protecting Behaviors, he never got any of the Real Love he badly needed. In fact, his behavior exhausted him, made loving relationships impossible, and left him empty and alone. For Matthew—as for all of us—Getting and Protecting Behaviors proved to be both fruitless and counterproductive. When we understand that, we can begin to consciously abandon them and make wiser choices in our lives.

Each time I tell the story of Matthew or of others like him, someone wonders aloud, "But what about the many times when Matthew's parents *did* love him? Don't those count? Why did he grow up empty and afraid just because there were a few times when they were critical?"

To answer these questions, I ask you to imagine that when you and I meet for the first time, we only have ten minutes to spend together. For the first nine minutes, our conversation is delightful and you feel warmly accepted by me. But during the last minute, I scream at you and chase you around the room with a butcher knife. What is the overall effect? Do you remember only our first nine minutes together and feel loved and safe with me? Of course not. The effects of fear and pain are overwhelming. Until a child—or an adult—is utterly convinced that he or she is loved unconditionally, even a small amount of doubt or fear is sufficient to destroy the effect of many moments of acceptance and safety.

All of us have received time, praise, and attention from our parents and others, but if that was conditional, it felt very unfulfilling to us, whether we realized it at the time or not. Only Real Love can create the connection to other people that makes us genuinely happy.

Again, I choose to believe that our parents gave us the best they had. If they didn't give us Real Love, it was only because they didn't receive it themselves and were empty and afraid. They were so preoccupied with their own needs and fears that they were unable to genuinely care about our happiness. But the result, intentional or not, is that we are then unable to give Real Love to our own children and others, and so the cycle continues, from one generation to the next, until we learn how to change our behaviors.

"I Love You Because . . ."

When two people fall in love, each one is likely to tell the other what it is about him or her that is so "lovable." We all like to hear that we're intelligent or handsome or beautiful or witty or dependable, but ironically, those are just the kinds of statements that cause relationships to fail. We don't realize that when we say we love our partner *because* of some particular characteristic or behavior, we're also indicating that we expect him or her to maintain that characteristic or behavior in order to retain our love. Our expression of love is often an expression of expectation, and if our partner lets us down, we become disappointed or irritated and demonstrate the conditional nature of our love.

We have thoroughly romanticized the idea of falling in love. We hope that falling in love will magically rescue us from all our problems, without any real effort on our part. The truth about falling in love is much less romantic than the myth, but if we honestly examine the truth, we can avoid the inevitable pain of "falling out" of love.

When we feel empty and alone, we're desperate for something or someone to make us happy. If we find someone who possesses qualities we like, and if he or she shares those qualities with us, we feel wonderful and say that we "love" that partner. We have found in him or her a source of Imitation Love (praise, power, pleasure, safety). Unconsciously, we then use a variety of Getting Behaviors to ensure that our partner will continue to give us the Imitation Love we want. Of course, our partner wants a relatively equal supply of Imitation Love in exchange, and if we can work out a trade that's equitable and abundant, the two of us declare that we are "in love."

It may not be very romantic, but that's what it means when *most* people say they're "in love." Inevitably, however, one or both of two things happen: First, one partner might fail to keep up his or her end of the trade. If you sense that you're giving your partner the same praise and pleasure as always, while he or she is contributing less to the relationship, that perception of inequality tends to cause contention and dim the rosy glow of romance. Second, the effect of Imitation Love always wears off, leaving both partners disillusioned. No amount of Imitation Love can ever give us the genuine happiness we hoped it would, and when it fails to live up to our expectations, we unfortunately place the blame on our partner. And because we don't understand what's happening when we fall in and out of love, we condemn ourselves to repeat the same frustrating and destructive pattern forever.

When two people are in love, they're quite sincere when they say, "I love you," but if they understood what was truly happening, they would say this: "Really loving you would mean caring about *your* happiness, but I care a lot more about how *I* feel. I like it when you do what *I* want. When you listen to me, I feel flattered and important. When you spend time with me, I don't feel as empty and alone. I feel good when I'm with you." When we don't feel unconditionally loved and we tell someone we love him, we're only expressing a selfish wish for that person to keep making *us* feel good. But when we say, "I love you," our partner hears us promise that we'll make *him* or *her* happy. Those conflicting expectations cause the failure of most relationships, which is what happened in the case of Diane and Frank.

> For most of us, the real meaning of "I've fallen in love" is "I've found someone who will give me all the Imitation Love I want."

When they met, Frank was a forklift operator in a carpet factory. He was a "guy's guy," who loved football, hated school, and avoided "sissy stuff" like dancing at all costs. But because he was attracted to Diane, he wanted to please her. So when she told him she loved to dance, and asked if he did, too, he lied. He told her what he knew she wanted to hear and made a date to take her dancing.

On their first date, Diane talked about how much she'd enjoyed college and valued intellectual pursuits. When she asked what kind of work he did, Frank said he was a supervisor in a carpet factory and that he was planning to go back to school to finish his degree—more lies.

Although Frank and Diane were different in many ways, they might still have had a good relationship if it hadn't been for Frank's poor choices. His lies weren't intended to hurt Diane, but because he'd never felt loved unconditionally himself, he felt empty and afraid, and therefore couldn't stop himself from trying to make her like him. His experience had taught him that love had to be earned, and that often means pretending to be what you think someone else wants you to be. As a result, he mistakenly thought he could build a relationship by pretending to be what she liked, and the results were predictable.

Diane hadn't felt loved unconditionally, either, and she hoped Frank would make her happy. So, even though she sensed that he wasn't really enthusiastic about school, and it was obvious that he rarely danced, she was flattered by his efforts to please her. In other words, she was aware that he might be lying, but because his lies benefited her, she went along with them willingly.

Soon after Frank and Diane got married, they began to tire of trading Imitation Love, and as always happens, its effects began to wear thin. Frank never did go back to school and he never again took Diane dancing. She began to fear that she'd made a terrible mistake, and her initial reaction to that fear was to lie to herself by pretending it didn't matter. But eventually her disappointment became unbearable and she chose to attack Frank by angrily reminding him about his many broken promises. At least when she was angry she got his attention, which made her feel temporarily less helpless and ignored. But what she felt certainly wasn't love.

Then, when attacking didn't work, she unconsciously changed her approach and began to act like a victim. She'd burst into tears during arguments, and on those few occasions when her tears actually did get her what she wanted—for the moment—she became clingy and effusively grateful.

Eventually, all Frank and Diane's Getting and Protecting Behaviors failed to produce love or happiness, and they simply began to avoid each other, running from the relationship. When they finally divorced, neither of them was any the wiser about the reasons their relationship had failed, and so, sad to say, they were doomed to repeat their mistakes.

Diane and Frank had both done the best they knew as they tried to make their relationship work, but because neither of them had experienced Real Love, they simply didn't know how to give or receive it. They didn't consciously *want* to make bad choices, but the choices they made were based on their own experience and were, therefore, the only choices available to them. You can't give bread to a starving man if you don't have any yourself. But fortunately, in the case of Real Love, it is possible to go out and get some, and as your own supply increases, you'll have more of it to give.

Making Choices

When some people hear that the lack of Real Love leads to the use of Getting and Protecting Behaviors—as in the case of Diane and Frank—they ask questions like the following: "Are you suggesting that just because Diane and Frank were unloved as children, they didn't have any control over their own behavior after that? If we didn't get Real Love as children, are we all doomed? Can we use the lack of Real Love as an excuse for every mistake we make? Don't we still have the ability to make our own choices?"

Many other authors have wisely written about our ability to determine our own feelings and behavior. They speak of our personal power, self-control, self-determination, and ability to be proactive. And they're quite right to say that we human beings do have a unique ability to comprehend, be self-aware, and make self-determining decisions; and they correctly point out that we tend to falsely blame our partners for feelings and situations that were largely of our own choosing.

Even with our wondrous capacity for comprehension and self-determination, however, it would be naïve to believe that our choices are not profoundly influenced by all the things that have happened to us. Let's suppose that a man is starving to death through no fault of his own—perhaps there is a widespread famine. Obviously, he can't run as quickly or work as hard as he could when he was healthy and eating well. It would be untrue—and unkind—for us to suggest that such a man *chooses* to run slowly. It would be insensitive to tell him that if only he'd exercise more self-control or be more proactive, he would suddenly be able to run faster. He needs more from us than the encouragement to make a different choice.

Similarly, people who are raised with insufficient Real Love don't *choose* to be empty and afraid, but they are. And in that condition, they *will* choose Getting and Protecting Behaviors, because they're emotionally and spiritually starving, and they *cannot* be as loving or happy as those who have received sufficient unconditional love all their lives. Fortunately, however, we can all learn to change our feelings and behaviors. Helping us to do that is my entire purpose for writing this book.

During the process of that learning experience, we can to some extent exert simple self-control over our Getting and Protecting Behaviors even before we feel unconditionally loved. Because we have a conscience, the ability to see that we are causing harm, and the ability to make decisions, we can comprehend that lying and anger—I'm just picking two examples here of Getting and Protecting Behaviors—cause unhappiness for us and for those around us. Even without feeling loved, we can see that these behaviors are unproductive, and we can then make a decision to stop using them. In fact, making conscious decisions to stop using Getting and Protecting Behaviors and to be more loving toward people, even when we don't feel sufficiently loving ourselves, can contribute significantly to the process of feeling loved and being loving.

Why then do I emphasize the role of Real Love—as compared to self-control—for eliminating Getting and Protecting Behaviors? Because for many years I have watched people struggle with all their might to control behaviors that were destroying their happiness and their relationships. They've put their whole hearts and souls into their efforts, and still they have failed. Simply exercising their will was not enough. Like the starving man, they needed more than self-control. And I have then watched those same people completely change their lives with relative ease when they felt unconditionally loved. Real Love and self-control actually work together in a powerful way, which is something we'll discuss in Chapter Four.

Years ago I had a problem with an unwanted vine in my yard that spread all over the place. When I pulled it out, it grew right back. In fact, it seemed to grow faster than before. I discovered that I couldn't get rid of it permanently until I found a long, narrow shovel that eliminated the roots. Similarly, if we want to get rid of Getting and Protecting Behaviors, we have to eliminate the root cause, which is the lack of Real Love. We may have occasional success with pulling up the leaves and stems—using self-control and other techniques—but real success will come only when we treat the roots.

Changing Our Choices

I enjoy splitting wood, and for years I used an ax to do the job. An ax can easily split soft wood, like pine, but it gets stuck in hardwoods, like oak. Splitting some kinds of logs with an ax is actually impossible. One day I was in a hardware store and saw something that looked like an ax, but it was thicker and heavier. They called it a maul. I took it home and could not believe how easily I split oak logs that had thoroughly exhausted me before.

I initially *chose* to split logs with an ax. *From the choices I could see at the time*—a shovel, an ax, or my bare hands—the ax was clearly the best. A maul would have worked much better, but I didn't know it existed. After learning about it, I was able to choose a superior tool for splitting wood.

Similarly, it is true that we always have choices about how we feel and behave. But when we don't feel unconditionally loved, *the choices we see* may be severely limited. When we're empty and afraid, Getting and Protecting Behaviors may be the only choices we can see or have the ability to make. If we've never seen Real Love, we don't even know that being loving exists as a choice for us in a given situation. And even after Real Love has been described to us, we may *see* it as a choice but still be incapable of *making* the loving choice, because we don't actually have the love to give. As we find Real Love and feel it, we are able to make new choices—loving, happy choices.

Although I emphasize that the lack of Real Love causes the emptiness and fear that lead to our Getting and Protecting Behaviors, I intend that to be an *explanation* for our behaviors, not an *excuse* for continuing them. Even when we feel unloved and unhappy, it is always *our* responsibility to learn what we can do to change our choices. And as we make wiser choices in our lives, we will be able to avoid the unproductive decisions of the past and will find the love and happiness we seek.

Being Seen and Getting Loved

The Tale of the Wart King and the Wise Man

If most of us have never experienced either giving or receiving Real Love, how do we learn to recognize it and begin to make the choices that will bring it into our lives?

This can happen for all of us, and the following story will help to explain how.

The Tale of the Wart King and the Wise Man

Once there was a rich and beautiful kingdom that stretched beyond the horizon in all directions. But the prince of that kingdom was very unhappy. He had warts all over his face, and everywhere he went, people teased him and laughed at him. So he mostly stayed in his room, alone and miserable.

Upon the death of his father, the prince became king and issued a decree that no one—on pain of death—would ever laugh at his warts again. But still he stayed in his room, ashamed and alone. On the rare occasions that he did go out, he put a cloth bag over his head, which covered his warts but also made it difficult for him to see.

Finally, after many years, the king heard about a Wise Man living on top of a nearby mountain. Hoping the Wise Man could help him, the king climbed the mountain and found the old man sitting under a tree. Taking the bag off his head, the king said, "I've come for your help."

The Wise Man looked intently at the king for several long moments and finally said, "You have warts on your face."

The king was enraged. That was not what he'd climbed all that way to hear. "No, I don't," he screamed. Ashamed and angry, he put the bag back over his head.

"Yes, you do," the Wise Man insisted gently.

"I'll have you killed!" shouted the king.

"Then call your guards," the Wise Man said.

"My guards aren't here!" the king shrieked helplessly. "I climbed all the way up this mountain to ask for your help, and all you can say is that I have warts on my face?! How cruel you are!"

Angry and frustrated, the king ran from the Wise Man, falling repeatedly because he couldn't see very well with the bag on his head. Finally, the king fell down a steep slope and into a lake, where he began to drown. The Wise Man jumped in, pulled the king to shore, and took the bag from his head so he could breathe.

The king was horrified when he saw the Wise Man staring at him. "You're laughing at me," the king said.

"Not at all," the Wise Man replied, smiling.

With his eyes fixed on the ground, the king said, "The boys in the village laughed at me, and my father was ashamed of me."

"I'm not one of the boys in the village," the Wise Man immediately responded, "and I'm not your father. That must have been hard for you."

"Yes, it was," the king admitted, with tears in his eyes.

"But as you can see, I'm not laughing at you, and I'm not ashamed of you," the Wise Man repeated.

Somehow being with the Wise Man did feel different to the king. He looked into the lake and saw his reflection. "I really do have a lot of warts."

"I know," the Wise Man agreed.

"And you don't find them disgusting?"

"No, and I don't find my own warts disgusting anymore, either."

The king noticed for the first time that the Wise Man also had warts. "Why do *you* not wear a bag over your head?"

"I used to," the old man replied, "but with the bag over my head, I couldn't see. And I was lonely. So I took it off."

"Didn't people laugh at you?" asked the king.

"Oh, sure, some did. And I hated that, just as you do. But gradually I found a few people who didn't laugh, and that made me very happy."

The king was thrilled. No one had ever looked at his warts without laughing at him or showing their disgust. "I think I won't wear the bag when you're around."

The Wise Man smiled. "When you go home, you might even leave the bag here."

"Will I find other people like you, who won't think I'm disgusting?" the king wondered aloud.

The Wise Man nodded. "Of course you will. And with the love of those people, you won't care when other people laugh."

The king dropped the bag on the ground and went back to his kingdom, which was far more beautiful without the bag over his head. And he did find people who didn't mind his warts at all. For the first time in his life, he was very happy.

How to Recognize and Find Real Love:
Truth → Seen → Accepted → Loved

Like the Wart King, most of us have learned from experience that people express their affection far less when they see our many mistakes and flaws, especially the ones that inconvenience them. So we lie by hiding our flaws, which enables us to avoid criticism; but doing that also makes it impossible for people to see who we really are. By hiding under the bags we've put on our heads, and using our other Getting and Protecting Behaviors, we briefly feel safer and "happier," but these behaviors actually keep us alone and prevent us from recognizing Real Love even when it's being given.

Remember that Real Love is always a gift freely given and freely received. It's Real Love when someone cares about your happiness with no thought for what he or she might get in return. It's a genuine caring that cannot be bought, traded, manipulated, or forced. When we do *anything* to get people to like us (Getting Behaviors) or to hurt us less (Protecting Behaviors), we cannot feel that what we receive is being freely offered, and so we can only experience it as Imitation Love—even in those rare instances when we're actually being offered Real Love, despite our manipulation.

Imagine this scenario: You look out your window and see a man walking toward your house carrying a bushel of apples. You want some of those apples, so you hurry outside and say, "I haven't had a bite to eat all day, and no one will give me anything." The first statement is a lie and the second presents you as a victim.

The man with the apples starts to say something, but you

don't wait to hear what it is. Instead, you rush on, verbally attacking him and making him feel guilty. "I hope you remember all the things I've done for you in the past."

The man then gives you the apples, but what you don't know is that he'd actually picked them specifically from his orchard to give to you as a gift. The apples may taste good, but they can't make you feel loved, because you know that you manipulated the man into giving them to you.

Real Love can only be *felt* when it's freely offered and received. Although the man *offered* his gift freely (Real Love), you did not *receive* it freely. In effect, you *bought* the apples with your behavior—by lying, acting like a victim, and attacking—just as if you'd paid for them with money. And because of what you did, whatever the man gave you could not *feel* like a gift. If you'd only allowed him to offer the apples without your doing or saying anything beforehand, your feelings about his gift would have been entirely different. You would have *felt* his unconditional concern for you. You've transformed any possibility of Real Love into Imitation Love, like turning gold into lead—a most unproductive reverse alchemy. This is what happens whenever we do anything to manipulate another person into giving us something we think we want, such as praise, attention, approval, and sex. Whatever we receive will always feel purchased and less worthwhile, even if it was freely offered.

The danger in this is that, if we don't learn to distinguish between the two, we can easily be satisfied by the deceptive

> When you use Getting and Protecting Behaviors, you will not be able to feel Real Love, even when it's being given to you.

pleasures of Imitation Love, which might utterly prevent us from finding the Real Love that makes life worth living. That is the real danger of Imitation Love, that it seductively leads us away from the true source of happiness.

Only when we set aside our Getting and Protecting Behaviors and tell the *truth* about ourselves can we create an opportunity for others to see us as we really are. Only when we are *seen* can we feel genuinely *accepted* and believe that other people truly care about *our* happiness, which is the definition of *Real Love*. It's a simple but powerful process—Truth → Seen → Accepted → Loved—the power of which the Wart King discovered when he told the truth about himself to the Wise Man. Only when we take the bags off our heads—when we tell the truth about ourselves, especially about our mistakes and flaws—can we feel unconditionally accepted and loved. The effect of Real Love is miraculous, even when we feel accepted and loved for only short periods of time: We lose our emptiness and fear, and when that happens, we gradually lose our need for those self-destructive Getting and Protecting Behaviors. Once we've tasted the Real thing, Imitation Love no longer has the same power to seduce and distract us, and we're finally able to share the love we have with others and participate in loving relationships.

Wise men (or women) are those people who function for us as the Wise Man did for the Wart King—people who feel sufficiently loved themselves that they're capable of accepting and loving us when they see the truth about us. I'll be using the term *wise man* often as we talk more about how to go about finding these people. Eventually, we can all become loving enough to be wise men and women for each other.

The best way to become familiar with Real Love is, quite simply, to experience it consistently so you get to know what

> ◌ When you tell the truth about yourself, you create
> the opportunity to find someone who will
> unconditionally accept you, just as the Wise Man did for
> the Wart King:
>
> > Truth → Seen → Accepted → Loved

it *feels* like. Once you know that, it's difficult to be deceived
by imitations. But in order to become familiar with Real
Love, you must first be willing to tell the truth about yourself.

Fortunately, even before we've become familiar with the
feeling of Real Love, we can look for two characteristics that
reliably identify it:

1. *The absence of Getting and Protecting Behaviors.* If you're
   using these behaviors, you can't be feeling Real Love, nor
   can you be concerned about the happiness of your partner.
   If your partner is using these behaviors, he or she is interested only in his own needs, not yours.
2. *The absence of disappointment, anger, and fear.* As we discussed in Chapter One, disappointment and anger indi-
   cate that we're concerned for our own happiness, not that
   of our partner. When we have these feelings, we can't be
   giving Real Love to anyone. When people are empty and
   afraid, they can only be concerned about what others will
   do *for* them or *to* them. They can't be concerned for the
   genuine happiness of anyone else.

As you learn more about the characteristics of Real Love,
begin to tell the truth about yourself, and experience unconditional acceptance, it will become increasingly easier for you
to recognize and find Real Love.

The Truth About Relationships and Individual Choices

The reason for learning to recognize and find Real Love isn't abstract or theoretical; we need to learn these things because Real Love actually transforms our lives by enriching our relationships with everyone around us on a daily basis.

In school, I had to learn geometry, chemistry, and history, even though I now can't recall the last time anyone asked me to calculate the hypotenuse of a triangle, diagram the steps of the Krebs citric acid cycle, or describe the significance of the Council of Trent in European history. Most of us, in fact, have spent many years studying subjects in school that we rarely use, while we were taught nothing at all about relationships, a subject we're required to deal with every day.

The most fundamental principle of all relationships is the Law of Choice, which states that everyone has the right to choose what he or she says and does. Nothing is more important than our ability to make independent choices for ourselves. Imagine what our lives would be like if that right were taken from us. We wouldn't be individuals at all, only meaningless tools in the hands of those who made our choices for us. *A relationship is the natural result of people making independent choices.*

Just as a painting is composed of countless individual brushstrokes, so it is that who we are is a result of all the choices we've made over a lifetime. Every decision has left us more

---

The Law of Choice: *Everyone has the right to choose what he or she says and does.* A relationship is the natural result of people making independent choices.

alone or loved, angry or happy, weak or strong. In our infancy, other people may have applied those strokes to the canvas of our lives, but with time we increasingly took the brush into our own hands. And from all those choices, we've created a canvas with a unique color that includes our personality, style, needs, fears, and even our Getting and Protecting Behaviors.

When we mix blue and yellow paint, the *natural result* is green. Green isn't something we hope for or even work for. It just happens *every time* we mix blue and yellow. Similarly, relationships naturally result from the blending of the colors of each partner, colors produced by the choices each partner has made independently over a lifetime. If I'm yellow and you're blue, our relationship will be green. It doesn't matter that I *want* our relationship to be orange, or that you want it to be turquoise. The result *will be* green.

Our relationships, therefore, are often not what we expect or want them to be, just as expectations and desires are completely irrelevant to the result we achieve when we mix two different colors. Relationships can only be the result of the *choices we've already made.* If two people have been unconditionally loved and have made a lifetime of unconditionally loving choices, they *will* have a mutually loving relationship. If, however, they have not been unconditionally loved, they *will* choose to get Imitation Love and protect themselves, and as a result of those choices, their relationship *cannot* be loving. They can, however, learn to find Real Love and introduce that into their relationship.

In any relationship, we have what amount to four basic choices to make independently: to change our partner; to live with it and like it; to live with it and hate it; or to leave.

Here's how those choices applied to the relationship between Joan and Tyler. Joan was angry with her husband,

Tyler, because, no matter how much she begged and nagged him, he never picked up after himself, and his messiness had eventually become more than she could stand. She finally talked about the situation to a wise friend. Remember, as I said earlier in the chapter, that a wise man is *anyone* who feels sufficiently loved in a given moment that he or she is capable of accepting and loving us when he sees the truth about us. All of us have wise friends around us, and I'll be talking more about how to find them in the following chapter.

"The man lives like a pig," Joan angrily complained to her wise friend. "He throws his stuff all over the floor and then I have to clean up after him. It doesn't matter how many times I talk to him—he never listens."

"So," said the wise man, "you expect Tyler to be neater and more considerate of you, is that right?"

When Joan agreed, her friend went on. "Then your relationship is doomed. Relationships result from the choices people make independently. Tyler has chosen to be a pig, and he gets to make that choice, even if it's inconvenient for you. He's almost certainly been a pig all his life, long before he met you. But you're not a helpless victim here. You still have your own choices to make."

Joan, naturally curious, asked what those choices might be.

"As I see it, you can make one of three: live with the pig and like it, live with the pig and hate it, or leave the pig."

"But—" Joan protested.

"There is no *but*," the wise friend interjected. "You want a fourth choice, which would be to stop him from being a pig, but that's not your choice to make, because it would be violating Tyler's right to choose. Even when what we want is good, and other people make bad choices, we can't *make* them do what we want. You only get to make choices that involve your own behavior."

Like Joan, most of us, when we're dissatisfied with our partner in any way, want to change him or her. But as I've said, relationships aren't based on what we want; they're determined by the choices each of us has already made individually.

The Worst Choice: The Nonchoice

We usually like *some* things about our partner, or else we'd never have begun the relationship in the first place. And even though we're aware from the beginning that there are also things we don't like, we simply assume we'll be able to change them— much as we'd rearrange a roomful of furniture. But that's not Real Love. Trying to change another person is manipulative, controlling, and arrogant, and it proves that we're primarily concerned with our own happiness, not our partner's. And, in any case, because that other person's attitudes and behaviors are the result of his own lifetime of experience, they're almost impossible to change.

With enormous effort and persistence, it is possible to change some things about another person. Some of us attack people or play the victim so effectively that we really can get our partners to behave differently. But even if we do that, our victory must be hollow, because anything we get as a result of manipulation cannot be felt as Real Love and is therefore worthless.

———

There were times when Joan's nagging and blaming were so unbearable to Tyler that he actually did clean up his mess. When that happened, Joan thought she was getting what she wanted, but what a price she paid! He resented her, and because his cooperation was not freely offered, she never felt loved. But even if Tyler had cleaned up his mess as an act of Real Love freely given, Joan would not have been able to feel it, because she'd manipulated him with her Getting Behavior.

In fact, by controlling Tyler, Joan was making sure she would feel alone. By manipulating him, she was depriving him of the ability to make independent choices, of showing his "true colors," which means that she was not having a relationship with the person Tyler really was. He became nothing more than an extension of *her* will—and so she was alone. Whenever we control another person, that person becomes nothing more than an object—no different from our shoes or our car—and we can't have a relationship with an object. I spend a lot of time with my shoes and my car every day, but when I'm with them, I'm still alone.

But perhaps the worst consequence of controlling others is that we can't learn to be loving, which is the greatest joy of all. We can't be happy while we're selfishly manipulating people.

Expectations, a Close Cousin to Controlling

Although many of us would deny that we're trying to control our partners—we may not make overt demands like Joan, for example—most of us still have enormous *expectations* of them, and those expectations can cause as much harm in our relationships as outright manipulation.

When we don't feel unconditionally loved, we experience so much emptiness and pain that we understandably turn to our partners in the expectation that they will do something to help us. Sometimes we believe our expectations are justified because we've given something—our time and attention, for example—to that other person. In other words, we think we have the right to expect something because we've *paid* for it. Sadly, that way of thinking only leads to the situation that exists in most relationships: "I'll give you what you want if you give me what I want." It's a *trading* of Imitation Love. That may satisfy both partners temporarily, but no relationship can be genuinely fulfilling when it's based on trading rather than unconditional giving.

For example, if you bring home flowers and tell your wife you love her, but then you expect sex in return, you're just giving her praise and power in exchange for pleasure and power for yourself. Early in a relationship, that may create a feeling of superficial happiness, but it doesn't last long, and eventually the unfulfilled expectations cause nothing but contention. If you perform an act of service for your husband, but you have expectations of praise and gratitude for what you do, you'll feel only an increase in the tension of your relationship. Although you may not openly nag your partner to get what you want, honestly ask yourself what you expect your partner to do for you. Is it to be grateful for everything you do for him or her, to compliment you on your appearance, take the major responsibility for the household chores, take care of you when you're sick, read your mind and be extrasensitive to you when you're in a bad mood, have sex on demand, be nice to your difficult parents, do the disciplining of the children, handle the family finances, and so on? If you have these expectations, and others like them, your partner will feel the pressure of them.

And so, while we may avoid the pitfall of direct manipulation, we can still destroy our relationships if we crush our partners under the burden of our expectations. Expectations cannot be justified either by what we need or by what we have done for others. The Law of Expectations, which follows naturally from the Law of Choice, states that *we never have the right to expect that another person will do anything for us.* If each partner in a relationship truly allows the other the right to make his or her own choices, neither one can ever have the right to *expect* the other to do *anything.* How arrogant it would be for me to expect that you would change who you are just for my convenience. Surely you wouldn't expect that of your partner. And yet that's just what you do every time you're angry or disappointed with anyone—you're indicating that your expectations have not been met. Most of us have these expectations all the time. We expect our spouses, our children, our bosses, our co-workers, and even other drivers on the road to change their behavior—to change who they are—in order to make our lives more convenient. Expectations are self-serving and unloving—and therefore they are "wrong," as we defined that word at the end of Chapter One.

Whenever we expect another person to change in any way, we are, in effect, demanding that he or she love us—care about us—and make us happy. But Real Love can never be demanded; it can only be freely given and received. And so, as in the case of the apples, any love we demand can never be felt as Real, even if it is. Our expectations seriously interfere with our happiness.

> The Law of Expectations: *We never have the right to expect that another person will do anything for us.* Expectations lead to disappointment, anger, and unhappiness in relationships.

The only exception to the Law of Expectations occurs in the case of a *promise,* which is an agreement on the part of one person to perform a specific act. Whereas expectations are destructive in loving relationships, they are an accepted part of any promise. If I promise my wife to pick up our daughter after school, she has a right to expect me to fulfill that promise.

It may seem strange to state the Law of Expectations so

categorically—"We *never* have the right to expect that another person will do *anything* for us"—and then immediately to claim promises as an exception. I do that because I want to emphasize that expectations are terribly damaging to relationships. When we have expectations of our partners, we set ourselves up for the inevitable disappointment and anger that make loving relationships impossible. And so, as a general rule, we need to diligently avoid expectations and only rarely justify an expectation with a claim that our partner has made a promise.

What kind of expectations *are* acceptable in a relationship? We can have expectations about many things, *but we never have the right to expect someone to love us or make us happy, even when they promise to do so*—as in the case of wedding vows. When marriages have problems, one spouse (or both) often says, "When we got married, we promised to love, cherish, and honor each other, right there in front of God and everybody—and my spouse isn't keeping his (or her) end of the agreement." While it's true that I may *promise* to love you, the moment you *expect* me to keep that promise, you destroy the possibility of feeling *unconditionally* accepted, because unconditional love can only be freely given *and* freely received. When we *expect* love, anything we receive can only feel like an order that was filled, or something we paid for.

At this point, many people wonder why they should ever get married. What's the purpose of wedding vows if they can't expect their spouse to love them? The principal reason many people get married is so they *can* have an expectation that someone will love them for the rest of their life. And so, if, as I've said, expectations are unproductive, marriage might seem like a bad idea altogether. For now, let me say that when we stop seeing marriage as an obligation for our partner to fill our expectations, and instead see it as an opportunity to learn to love another person, it becomes the most beautiful experience imaginable. We'll talk much more about the purposes of marriage in Chapter Eight, after laying a foundation for it in the following chapters.

With the exception of love and happiness, you can expect your partner to fulfill almost any kind of promise: take out the garbage, support the family financially, stay home and raise the children, clean the kitchen, do the shopping, and so on. However, the promise needs to be *clearly understood by both parties*. You cannot expect your partner to do something just because you think he *should*. In the case of Joan and Tyler, Tyler did not promise to pick up his clothes before he married Joan, so she had no right to expect him to do that. But the real problem was that, because Joan had insufficient Real Love in her life, she expected Tyler to pick up after himself *as an indication that he loved her*—and she didn't have a right to expect that. In all unhappy relationships, the real cause of unhappiness is a lack of unconditional love; controlling and expectations are just symptoms of that cause.

What can you do when promises are violated, as they so often are? If Tyler *had* promised to pick up after himself, and then failed to do so, would Joan have been justified in being angry at him? *No*—because, as we've discussed, our ultimate purpose here is to be loved, loving, and happy, and anything that interferes with achieving that purpose is wrong. Being angry certainly qualifies in every way as wrong, since it has such a uniformly destructive effect on our ability to feel unconditionally loved and on our ability to love other people. And so, no matter what our partner does, we can never justify being angry—the consequences of anger are just too severe. Anger is always wrong.

So what *is* a productive reaction to a broken promise? Eric and Hannah, another married couple, demonstrate one such response. Hannah's brother was planning to buy a used car in three weeks, and he needed a sheltered workplace where he could perform some repairs on the car's engine. Hannah volunteered the use of her garage and asked Eric the next day if he had any problem with that. Eric agreed to the arrangement and said he would finally clean out all the stuff that had been collecting there for years.

A week before the day that Hannah's brother was to arrive with the car, she could see that Eric hadn't even begun, and she knew he'd need at least a week to get the job done. So Hannah asked, "Do you remember that my brother is bringing that car into the garage one week from today?"

It is not the words that are important here. What's important is how and why Hannah said them. Hannah understood what we all must remember whenever we speak in a loving relationship: Happiness comes from telling the truth and loving your partner. The truth and Real Love can never be separated. Hannah wasn't trying to attack Eric, as she had done many times in the past—"See, you're not keeping your promise, as usual!"—but was really trying to help him avoid that feeling of last-minute panic she knew he hated. And Eric could feel her genuine concern for him.

However, Eric had put off cleaning out the garage for years because it was an exceptionally distasteful chore, and the day before the deadline he still hadn't done anything. Hannah spoke to him about it again. "The car arrives tomorrow and must be protected from the rain until my brother finishes working on it. What can I do to help you?"

Hannah simply told the truth about the situation and loved her husband. That's all Eric needed. He knew he'd made a mistake, and he started working on it immediately. He had to take a day off work to finish the job, and he had to borrow a tarp from a friend to cover the car for two days while it sat in the driveway. Hannah could certainly have attacked Eric with nagging and anger, *but to what end*? He wouldn't have understood his responsibility any better, nor performed more efficiently. In fact, we all perform better when we feel loved than we do when we feel attacked. And with anger Hannah would have done great damage to their relationship. A clean garage isn't much of a trophy when you realize that your partner hates to be around you. We must always remember that a promise is far less important than a loving relationship.

The Remaining Three Choices

Earlier, I said that when it comes to changing a relationship, we have four choices. It should be obvious by now that trying to change your partner is always the worst choice of all, because it will never be fruitful. In fact, it's such a bad choice that I refer to it as the nonchoice. That leaves us with three remaining options.

The Happy Choice—Live with It and Like It. Tyler's messiness was just one brushstroke among the thousands that had combined to create his own personal color. Instead of choosing to accept and enjoy the beauty of his overall canvas, Joan chose to be miserably distracted by one stroke that inconvenienced her. Most of us do this with our partners. Real Love is what we all really want from every relationship, but because we didn't receive enough of it, we can't possibly identify what produces genuine happiness. The reason we try to change our partners is because we've learned that Getting and Protecting Behaviors are the only way to relieve the emptiness and fear that are the legacy of Imitation Love—which is the only kind of love we've ever known. But as we begin to feel unconditionally loved, we begin to see people without the blinding effects of emptiness and fear, and then all human beings become beautiful to us and easy to accept just as they are. Right now that may sound like magic to you, but it really happens that way, and in the following chapters I'll suggest ways for you to learn how to find that love for yourself so that you'll no longer be emotionally starving and will be able to share what you've found with your partners.

The Angry Choice—Live with It and Hate It. Many of us have tried to change a partner so many times that we've finally become frustrated and quit trying. We stay in the relationship, but we continue to wish that our partner were different, and we resent him or her when he or she isn't. In effect, we choose to stay in a relationship where unhappiness is the only possibility. We *choose* to be miserable.

Although the angry choice is obviously foolish, it's one that too many of us make. What we have to remember is that anger is always a choice, not something other people "make" us feel. When we understand that, we can begin to choose differently. We are not lifeless objects to be acted upon, like shoes or cars. We have the ability to determine how we will react to events. However, in our defense, when we don't feel unconditionally loved, sometimes we don't *see* that we have a choice other than anger. Without Real Love, we're often not *able* to make the loving choice, even though that choice still exists. As we gain experience with Real Love, we can *learn* to choose to be loving instead of angry—which, incidentally, *proves* that anger is a choice we make, not something that other people *cause* us to feel.

The Final Choice—Leaving. We can always leave a relationship, emotionally or physically, and there are always two ways to do that—blaming and not.

When we leave a relationship and blame our unhappiness on our partner, we use all the Getting and Protecting Behaviors. It's obvious that we're running, but we're also lying, because we believe and tell others that *our partner* is at fault, when the real cause of our misery is the long-standing lack of Real Love in *our* lives and *our* inability to accept and love our partner. As we're blaming, we're using attacking as a Getting and Protecting Behavior, and we're also acting like a victim, because we invariably say things like "Look what he (or she) has done to me!"

Sometimes leaving a relationship is the best thing to do. While we're learning to be truthful about ourselves and feel loved, we may become so confused and threatened in the presence of a particular person that we automatically revert to the familiar use of Getting and Protecting Behaviors. When that's the case, it may be unwise to spend time with that person, but we need to admit that *we* are the problem. *We* are not loving enough to participate in a loving relationship with that particular person. We'll talk more about leaving relationships in Chapter Nine. It is never a decision to be taken lightly.

> In any relationship, you really have only three choices to make: live with it and like it, live with it and hate it, or leave.

The Difference Between Asking and Expecting

After reading the story of Joan and Tyler, and the choices available to people in a relationship, you might still be puzzled. What about Tyler? Wasn't he being selfish, too? Shouldn't he have cared enough about his wife's happiness to have made the effort to clean up after himself? Why is this all about Joan?

These questions may be reasonable, but in the end they're simply not productive, because they're motivated by a desire for equal justice (or blame) rather than the desire to become more loving. Joan's wise friend discussed *her* behavior and choices exclusively because he knew that trying to change Tyler would be futile for her. Had he been talking with Tyler, he would have discussed *his* behavior and choices, not Joan's.

Remember, we don't have the right to make a choice for anyone else. We need to focus on taking our own steps toward feeling loved and being loving. It's those choices that will bring us the greatest happiness. But, you might still be thinking, *Didn't Joan at least have the right to* ask *Tyler to pick up some of his mess now and then? Were her only choices really to live with it and like it or to leave the relationship?* (Note that I purposely left out choosing to change Tyler and choosing to live with it and hate it, because those choices are impossible and stupid, respectively.)

These are important questions. Many of us live with partners who really *choose* to not carry their share of the load in the relationship. It may seem extreme that our only choices are to either live with that or to leave the relationship, but not when we realize that there's a great deal we can do *while* we are "living with it and liking it." The two most important things we can do are to fill ourselves with Real Love and learn to make loving requests—in that order.

Joan certainly had the right to ask Tyler to pick up after himself, but if she were feeling less than unconditionally loving when she made that request, he would naturally feel attacked. He might give in from time to time just to get her off his back, or he might stubbornly ignore her (as he'd been doing all along), but, either way, their relationship could only be further damaged as a result. *After* we've found Real Love for ourselves, however, and have learned to be unconditionally loving, we *can* easily make requests of our partner, and if we do that in the presence of unconditional love—without expectations—the results are often delightful and productive.

It's important to make requests of our partners—otherwise, how would anything get done? We'll discuss how to make loving requests in Chapter Seven, but only after we've talked much more about how to find Real Love and share it with others. We need to be very familiar with loving before we start making requests of our partners. Otherwise, our requests will be accompanied by expectations, and when that happens, a request becomes a destructive demand. Never forget that it is far more important in any relationship to receive and give Real Love than it is to make a request or to demand that a partner keep a promise. In Chapter Six we'll discuss what Joan might do if Tyler never does pick up after himself.

Taking the Leap of Faith

Everyday Wise Men and How to Find Them

With Real Love, nothing else matters. Without it, nothing else is enough. There is nothing in the world that begins to compare with the joy of feeling loved and loving others. Fortunately, finding the unconditional love we need is easy if we consistently follow these simple steps:

- Have a desire to change
- Exercise faith
- Tell the truth about yourself
- Give up your Getting and Protecting Behaviors

I want to emphasize here that although I'll be discussing these steps in sequence, you won't necessarily be taking them that way. They're all inseparably, continuously, and beautifully interconnected, like the steps of a dance. As you find Real Love in your life, you'll take each of these steps again and again, using some more than others, but never neglecting any one of them. This process has been thoroughly tested. It works. Thousands of people have taken these steps and filled their lives with Real Love. As a result, they have found a joy in their relationships they never imagined possible.

Remember the Wart King

If you reconsider the "Tale of the Wart King and the Wise Man," you'll see that the Wart King followed all the steps in the process. He was miserable as long as he hid his warts (lying), felt sorry for himself (victim), and tried to control the people around him (attacking). But after many years of being lonely and unhappy, he finally had a desire to change his life, and he went to see the Wise Man. Because the Wart King had been laughed at all his life, he needed considerable faith in order to leave his room and visit the old man. When the Wise Man confronted him with the truth about his warts, the king's faith was overwhelmed, and he responded with all the Protecting Behaviors. But after experiencing once again the futility of those old responses, he summoned additional faith in the Wise Man and stopped using his Getting and Protecting Behaviors. As he told the truth about himself, he was able to feel the full effect of the old man's love. Each step was connected and synergistic: When he told the truth, he was also exercising faith, trying to change, and giving up his Getting and Protecting Behaviors; when he was trying to change, he was also exercising faith; and so on.

Being Patient—Don't Expect Brass Bands

As you begin your search for Real Love, don't be too impatient. It doesn't usually arrive instantly, by the truckload, in the form of some kind of romantic explosion, or accompanied by a brass band. Rather, you'll feel it in small doses, a cupful here and there, as you begin to experience subtle changes in the way you feel about people and things. As you continue to tell the truth about yourself to people who are capable of seeing you, you'll experience small moments of acceptance and peace that will increase with practice and experience. You'll feel less empty and afraid, and less angry at the people around you. Don't be discouraged if you don't feel a tidal wave of love as you take the first steps toward finding it. At times, you'll still become afraid and you'll go back to getting Imitation Love and protecting yourself. In those moments, you'll lose the feeling of being loved for a while. Don't give up. Keep taking the steps, and the feeling will come back.

As we feel unconditionally loved, we begin to experience the kind of happiness we've always wanted, the kind of joy that many of us have never known. Real Love changes the way we see everything around us. It satisfies our greatest need and eliminates our greatest fear. Real Love is the most valuable prize of all. No effort we make to find it is too great.

Having a Desire to Change

In physics, we learn a principle called inertia: Any object moving in a particular direction will tend to continue moving in that direction unless something changes its course. Similarly, if we don't have a strong desire to change our lives, and if we don't act upon that desire, we will stay the same. We will not become wiser, more loving, and happier simply by accident.

And so we need to identify the factors that destroy our desire to change, because those are the things that guarantee our stagnation and unhappiness. When an addict gets enough of his drug, he calls that happiness and never addresses the real problems in his life, the problems that led to his drug use in the first place. That superficial satisfaction is therefore fatal. People with enough Imitation Love also think they're happy and ignore what they really need in order to be genuinely happy. They see no reason to risk telling the truth and taking the other steps necessary to find Real Love, and their self-deception can be emotionally deadly, much as drugs can be physically deadly. All forms of Imitation Love are highly addictive and deceptive, just like cigarettes or cocaine.

One sure way to kill the possibility of healthy change is always needing to be right, and yet some of us find that habit almost impossible to give up. Jane, for example, was miserable, and her marriage was falling apart. When she spoke to a wise friend, she presented a pile of evidence blaming all her misery on her husband. But the wise woman simply asked Jane, "What are *you* willing to do to change your relationship?"

"I'd do anything to not feel like this," Jane replied.

"Then tell me how all the problems in your marriage are *your* fault," her friend suggested.

Jane couldn't do that, even after her friend helped her see that *she* was empty and afraid, and that she was using all the Getting and Protecting Behaviors as she interacted with her husband. Despite her claim that she was willing to do anything to change her relationship, Jane was not willing to admit she was wrong. It was too important to her to be right.

If you're unhappy in a relationship, you're always wrong. If you can remember that sentence, it will change your life. When you're unhappy, it means that *you* haven't yet done enough to feel unconditionally loved and loving. That doesn't make your partner *right;* it just means that your happiness is always in your own hands. You need to focus your attention entirely on what *you* can do to become more loved and loving, because that's what will make the greatest difference in your relationship and in your happiness, not what you do to change your partner. As long as we focus on being right—by which I don't mean choosing the correct thing to do, but insisting on the appearance of being correct while making our partners appear to be wrong—we waste our time, effort, and chance for happiness. That is not a wise choice.

For many of us, it's helpful to understand that being wrong doesn't make us bad. It's just the critical first step in telling the truth and finding Real Love in relationships. Some people seem to find it impossible to admit being wrong. Being right is a protective habit they will not give up. But such people aren't bad, they're just afraid and angry. They've become so familiar with Getting and Protecting Behaviors—being right is a combination of lying and attacking—that they're terrified to do anything different. These people need to understand that, even though their emptiness began in childhood, through no fault of their own, what they do about it now *is* their responsibility. We are all responsible for the next step we take in our lives.

> If you're unhappy in a relationship, you're always wrong. As long as you focus on being right, you're wasting your time, effort, and chance for happiness.

To those of you who can't seem to stop being right, I suggest this: When you're unhappy, *something* is obviously not working. You *may be* partly right about a particular situation, but *so what!?* Would you rather be right or happy? The only worthwhile goal in life is to find joy. Therefore, if what you're doing isn't giving you true joy, change it, even if you can find some tiny thing you're doing that's blameless. Being right is worthless. Being happy is everything.

Exercising Faith

It's understandable that, like the Wart King, most of us have been hiding who we really are all our lives. We've learned from long experience that when people see our mistakes and flaws, they painfully criticize us and withdraw from us. But responding with all the Getting and Protecting Behaviors has only made us more alone and unhappy.

So why do we keep using these behaviors? Why don't we do something different? *Because we can only do what we know.* We can't choose a different path in life until we can *see* it. And even as we learn about new things that *will* make us happier—like the principles in this book—we still tend to do the same old, ineffective things because the unknown scares us to death. We prefer to do what's *familiar,* even if it works poorly, rather than risk stepping out into the unknown, where we might look stupid and feel lost. That approach may seem unwise, but fear has long made a mockery of wisdom.

Faith is the act of consciously choosing to experience something we don't know. That choice exposes us to possible danger, but it also creates the opportunity to learn and grow. Only with faith can we find Real Love and genuine happiness.

Faith is much more than words. Faith means believing that something is true and then *acting* on that belief, despite our fears. It's easy to stand on the ground and express a belief in the safety of skydiving. But when we actually jump out of a plane at fifteen thousand feet, that's faith. Similarly, it's easy to talk about wanting to change our lives, but we have no faith until we actually tell the truth about ourselves as the Wart King did—especially in situations where people might criticize and reject us.

We can have faith in anything: a parachute, the stock market, God, or a person, among others. I'd like to talk about the importance of a few specific kinds of faith that are essential to our finding genuine happiness—faith that change is possible, faith in the truth and in finding Real Love, faith that people do their best, and faith in our partner.

Faith That Change Is Possible. Most of us are deeply discouraged after a lifetime of trying to find happiness with Getting and Protecting Behaviors and Imitation Love. After all that failure, it takes enormous faith to pick ourselves up once again and believe that we can find Real Love and happiness. Without that faith, however, we'll never take the risks or expend the effort required to tell the truth about ourselves. And then we're doomed to continue feeling unloved and alone.

Faith in the Truth and in Finding Real Love. Truth → Seen → Accepted → Loved. Only by telling the truth about ourselves can we create opportunities to feel accepted and loved. We can't *feel* loved if we manipulate people in any way. But the problem is that in the past, when people learned the truth about our mistakes and weaknesses, they often laughed at us, criticized us, punished us, and avoided us. We reacted by learning that when we lied, we often avoided the pain of criticism and rejection. It worked for us as children, so understandably, we continue to lie as adults. After all those negative experiences with the truth, we naturally believe the same unpleasant results will occur each time our flaws are exposed. In addition, we tend to lie because that's what we've seen everyone else do. We've encountered few, if any, people in our lives who consistently tell the truth about themselves.

That's why it takes faith to tell the truth about ourselves now. Having faith in the truth means being honest about

ourselves *even though we don't know what the results will be.*
It means continuing to tell the truth even when we're not certain we're being accepted. When you have faith in the truth
and in finding Real Love, you simply tell the truth and then
wait to receive the greatest gift of all, which is unconditional
love and genuine happiness.

If we're physically out of shape, achieving fitness takes time
and effort. We rarely feel a significant change in our overall
well-being the first time we exercise. As a matter of fact, it
may even be painful! Similarly, the first time we tell the truth
about ourselves, we may not feel a positive result. If that happens, without faith we'll give up. We won't be honest about
ourselves long enough to see the positive effect that always
follows—because we can't predict how long that will be.
Without faith, we become frightened at the first sign of criticism or discomfort and go back to lying and using our other
Getting and Protecting Behaviors. If we want to feel unconditional love, we must have faith and simply decide to *keep*
telling the truth even when we're not getting the immediate
results we hoped for.

Sometimes people *will* attack us when we tell the truth
about ourselves, but those people are just afraid and protecting themselves. Having faith in Real Love does not mean believing we'll be loved by every person we meet, because many
people are simply incapable of loving us at the moment we
choose. Faith means believing that when we consistently tell
the truth, *someone* will accept and love us—and someone
will. I've seen this confirmed too many times to ever doubt it
again.

Real Love is infinitely available. As we continue to tell the
truth about ourselves, and as we avoid lying and using the
other Getting and Protecting Behaviors, we *will* find people
who are capable of loving us. Sometimes that only happens

for moments at a time—and perhaps more slowly than we'd prefer—but if we're not defending ourselves, we'll feel those moments, and they will change our lives.

As we exercise this faith and feel the unconditional love that's available to all of us, we no longer have to insist that any particular person love us right now. If the next ten people I meet fail to accept me—even if they're critical and otherwise attacking—that doesn't bother me at all, because I have faith that other people *will* love me. There have been plenty of times when people *did* love me. It doesn't matter how many people don't love you, only that some people do. *With faith,* remembering that *one* person loves you can outweigh the effect of a thousand people criticizing you. Without faith, the effect of one critical person can be overwhelming.

> Faith is a decision you make to tell the truth about yourself even when you're still uncertain about what might happen.

Faith That People Do Their Best. I don't know anyone who would eat with pigs out of a trough in a muddy barnyard if he knew that a well-prepared meal was available on a table in a clean house—do you? And that's because we *really do tend to make the best choice we can see.*

When we're not being loving, it's because we simply don't see the availability of that choice. We haven't been taught *how* to be loving. We're incapable of doing what we've never been taught, and we can't give what we've never received.

The same is true of everyone else. When other people inconvenience us or get angry at us, they're just empty and afraid and protecting themselves. They can't give what *they've* never received either. But we get angry at people when they treat *us* badly. We treat them as though they were intentionally withholding something from us. We actually believe that other people choose to hurt us when they could just as easily choose to love us.

If you have any doubt that emptiness and fear are the cause of anger, the next time someone is angry at you—preferably someone you've known for a while—apologize for inconveniencing him, give him a big hug, and tell him you love him. But only if you mean it. As his emptiness and fear disappear, see how long his anger lasts. With their anger, people are only protecting themselves, and they're doing what they've seen everyone around them do in similar situations. That doesn't justify what they do, but it does explain it.

People who are angry at us are doing their best and simply *can't* love us as we'd like. They're doing all they can do. I've never met an angry person who was intentionally withholding a secret supply of love. When we understand that, it makes no sense for us to continue resenting angry people. And when we realize that, it becomes much easier for us to have faith in them and to have a loving relationship with them.

Is it possible that other people are sometimes *not* doing their best with us when they're angry and otherwise unloving? On some occasions, could they not have exercised more self-control and made our lives more pleasant? Of course, but we *cannot know* when those times are, and even if we knew, what would we do with that information? As we've already discussed, it's not our right to try to change other people. And in any case, focusing on our need for *other people* to change will only make *us* selfish, unloving, and unhappy. The only reason for us to think about what other people should do in the first place is that we are empty and afraid. In that condition, all we can see is what people can do *for* us or *to* us. When we're in pain, we naturally expect some relief from the people around us—how could they see our obvious distress and not offer to help us? We reason to ourselves that when someone doesn't help us—or worse, when someone inconveniences or attacks us—he or she must be hurting us intentionally and therefore must be "bad."

When we believe people are bad, we fear them, use them, and protect ourselves from them. That makes them—and us—feel even more empty, afraid, and alone. And then we all use more Getting and Protecting Behaviors. It's impossible to have loving relationships with people when we see them in that way. It is far more productive to have faith that people do their best, and in any case the evidence supports that belief.

Faith in Our Partner. "Trust is earned." We've all heard that said many times, usually in an accusing way to someone whose trustworthiness is in doubt. Those three words clearly demonstrate the destructive lack of faith we have in each other. Moreover, it's a deadly lie that we use only to hide our own fear and anger. When people say, "Trust is earned," what they really mean is this:

> "I'm empty and afraid. I've been used and hurt by people many times in the past, and I'm afraid that everyone I meet will do the same things to me. I therefore protect myself constantly until people individually *prove* that I don't need to be afraid of them."

That faithless and frightened view of the world guarantees that we'll use Protecting Behaviors, which can only lead to everyone's feeling more afraid, unloved, and alone.

When we require people to prove they're worth trusting, we naturally—and mostly unconsciously—look for evidence that they're *not*. That's understandable, since we're afraid of being hurt and are eager to protect ourselves. However, the consequences of that fearful and protective approach are terribly destructive to relationships and to our own happiness because:

1. We look for the slightest mistakes to justify our fears and prove that our suspicions were correct. But as the people around us learn to tell the truth and become loving, they *will* make mistakes. They have to. We can't require them to be flawless when they interact with *us*. When we feel unloved and empty, however, and when we have no faith in people, we see every mistake as a threat to our well-being. That outlook keeps us afraid of almost everyone we know, which makes loving relationships impossible.

2. We see mistakes where they don't exist. In the absence of Real Love, we see the potential for being hurt everywhere, even by people who are quite harmless. We tend to see what we're looking for.

As long as we assume that our partners are hurtful, they can never prove otherwise, because we will interpret everything they do in a negative way, confirming our critical assumptions about them. We do all this to protect ourselves, but ironically, our attitude only succeeds in hurting us. The more we protect ourselves, the more alone we feel, because we can't feel accepted and loved by people we fear. Loving relationships become much easier when we simply *choose* to have faith and trust people. Waiting for other people to change and make us feel safe is slow, lazy, and irresponsible. Here's a sad story that demonstrates how much difference choosing—or not choosing—to have faith in your partner can actually make in your life.

Ellen and Chris fell in love. Neither of them had been unconditionally loved, so they were thrilled with all the attention and acceptance they got from each other. They were certain that their love was genuine, but without prior experience with Real Love, they could only trade Imitation Love. When the excitement of approval, praise, and sex began to wear off—as it always does when those things are used as forms of Imitation Love—they became increasingly dissatisfied with each other.

Chris started to avoid Ellen (running), while Ellen demanded that Chris give her the same amount of attention he used to when they were dating (victim, attacking). Desperate to do something about their situation, Ellen invited a wise friend to help them, a man who had always been accepting and loving with each of them in the past. Remember, a wise man is anyone who feels loved enough that he or she can clearly see and accept another person.

Ellen was angry as she began the conversation. "We never talk anymore. We never do anything together."

"Why would I want to?" asked Chris. "You're angry and nag at me all the time."

"And you don't ever listen to me," Ellen replied hotly, "or spend time with me. If I don't get angry, I can't get you to do anything."

"See? That's what I mean. You're angry right now, and I hate talking to you when you're like that. Who wouldn't hate it?"

Chris and Ellen argued a little longer, each intent on proving that the other was at fault.

The wise man finally intervened. "Chris, it's clear that you do avoid Ellen. And I understand that. Ellen, you're obviously angry at Chris, probably even more when you're alone than here with me watching. And I understand that, too. But at this point we don't need to go over all the mistakes you've made. It's not helpful. The important question is this: Are you both willing to try something different that will change your relationship completely?"

Chris and Ellen immediately sensed that their friend had no interest in criticizing them. They *felt* his acceptance and desire to help them. That is the effect a wise man has on people.

The wise man explained that neither of them felt unconditionally loved, and they each saw that was true. All their lives, the pain of feeling unloved and empty had dictated their unproductive use of Getting and Protecting Behaviors. In the beginning of their relationship, they both understandably hoped that their partner would give them the happiness they didn't have. But without Real Love, they could only give each other Imitation Love, which never lasts. The wise man explained the process of learning to tell the truth about themselves and creating opportunities for people to accept them unconditionally. He gave them the names of some of his wise friends who were capable of loving them in that way, and he suggested that they practice telling the truth about themselves with those people every day. He also suggested that they try telling the truth to some of their own friends. They met again a week later, and the wise man asked what they had learned in the past week.

"Nothing's changed," Ellen said. "He still doesn't do anything with me."

"Did either of you talk to any of the people I recommended?" the wise man asked.

Chris had talked to several people, and as he told them the truth about his mistakes and fears, he felt accepted. He enjoyed that so much, he even had dinner with two of the men he'd spoken with on the phone. This was a new and exciting experience for him. He then tried to tell the truth about himself to Ellen, but those conversations had gone poorly. Ellen had not made any phone calls, nor had she met with any of the people the wise man had recommended.

"I'm happy for you, Chris," said the wise man. "It sounds like you had a good time."

"But he hasn't changed," objected Ellen. "He still avoids me all the time."

"Ellen," said the wise man, calmly, "Chris is trying something that's very different for him. He's trying to tell the truth about himself, but because he's just starting, he still makes lots of mistakes, especially with you. That's unavoidable as he learns to be truthful and loving. Now let's talk about you. What are *you* willing to do to have a better relationship with Chris?"

"But how can I do anything when *he*—" accused Ellen.

The wise man gently interrupted her. "We've already talked about Chris. He's taking the first steps toward changing his life. That's all he can do at the moment. But now we're talking about you. Until *you* make the decision to have faith in Chris and trust that he's doing his best to learn to tell the truth and love you—no matter how many mistakes he makes—your relationship with him can't go anywhere."

"Me?!" said Ellen. "You're saying this is *my* fault?"

"I didn't say anything about fault," replied the wise man. "Placing blame is useless. I'm talking about how *you* can move forward, be happier, and change your relationship."

"How can I have faith in him when he still avoids me and doesn't care about me?"

"That's why it's called faith. Faith means acting on a belief that doesn't yet have proof. If Chris has to *prove* that he's completely truthful and loving before you believe it and accept him, you'll never have a loving relationship with him. You'll never see the real changes in him, and he won't want to share them with you. You'll never really trust him until you simply choose to do so."

"You're suggesting," said Ellen, "that I trust him even when he's avoiding me and being angry at me?"

"Yes. Real faith means believing that he's doing his best to tell the truth and love you even though there are times when it appears he's not. Until you're willing to do that, your relationship won't change. Trust is *not* earned; it's given as a gift."

Ellen could not accept what the wise man was saying, but Chris did. He *chose* to have faith in people, and that decision changed his life. He continued to tell the truth about himself to several wise men and women, and he trusted them to love him. As he felt seen, accepted, and loved, he felt less needy and afraid. He began to experience a consistent happiness that replaced the fear and anger that had consumed him in the past. Seeing clearly, he also found it easier to accept Ellen and care about her happiness (Real Love).

Ellen, however, chose to keep insisting that "trust is earned." She never did tell the truth about her own mistakes and fears, and she remained alone and miserable.

A lack of faith in other people means that we remain doubtful and fearful, and that we continue to protect ourselves. And in that condition, loving relationships are impossible.

Faith is not a feeling. It's not wishing or hoping. It's a choice we make. With faith, we *choose* to believe something is true and then *behave* as though it were. Anything short of that is not faith and will not lead to growth or happy relationships.

Many people argue that they can't tell the truth about themselves *until* they feel loved and safe. But telling the truth about ourselves is required *before* we can feel loved. Faith precedes the miracle of love. We can choose to have faith that telling the truth will bring us Real Love and happiness, **or** we can choose to lie and thereby be certain that we'll stay unloved and unhappy. It's that simple.

Every time we interact with people, we make a choice whether or not to exercise faith. When someone attacks you—or when you think someone might—I suggest silently repeating the following series of thoughts:

1. "When I attack other people—which includes all the forms of anger—I'm simply afraid and protecting myself. My primary interest is not to hurt them."
2. "Other people attack me with the same motivation."
3. "In this moment, I choose to see that the person attacking me is simply feeling unloved and afraid. He's protecting himself or trying to get me to make him feel better."
4. "If I react by protecting myself from this person, I can't feel loved, loving, or happy, *and* he will become more afraid and more likely to protect himself."
5. "I choose to have faith that being truthful and accepting will be more effective than protecting myself. I already know that protecting myself doesn't work."

Admittedly, taking these steps will be far easier once you have already felt unconditionally accepted by one or more people. Initially, the thought of exercising faith instead of protecting yourself can be scary. You may worry that if you trust someone who is actually lying to you or attacking you, you'll be hurt. But the actual risk is small. Lying and protecting yourself can *only* produce the same old feelings of temporary safety and being alone. The chance of finding genuine happiness is zero. On the other hand, even though telling the truth might not be immediately rewarding, the chances it creates for finding Real Love and happiness are *always* greater than zero. *Someone* will eventually accept and love you for who you really are. That's worth any risk you take. How can you lose? And the reward for your faith is huge: You can finally feel loved and learn to love others, the greatest experience in the world. In short, you have nothing to lose when you exercise faith and tell the truth.

A wise man can help you find faith. As he offers his acceptance and love, you will learn, as the Wart King did, that the world is not uniformly critical and conditionally loving. Wise men and women provide the fertile soil for nurturing the seed of faith we need in order to believe that change is possible, and that we can be loved and loving instead of afraid, angry, and manipulating. A wise man introduces the possibility that truth can lead to love, and love to happiness. Faith is choosing to act on that possibility.

Telling the Truth About Yourself

Telling the truth about yourself is the most concrete, active step you can take in the process of finding Real Love. It's where the rubber meets the road. Carol found that out when she complained about her husband, James, to a wise friend.

"James is always—" Carol began, before her friend, who had heard it all before, interrupted.

"I've never seen you feel happier after complaining about James. Have *you?*"

Carol was surprised and confused. "Are you taking his side?"

The wise woman laughed. "Not at all. He probably does all the things you say and more, but be honest—has it ever made you or James genuinely happier when you complain about him?"

"But he—"

The wise woman interrupted again. "You can talk about

him all you want, but I care about you enough to say that talking about *him* won't help you."

"So what do I talk about?"

"Talk about yourself."

"Okay," said Carol. "*I* feel angry when James doesn't listen to me or care about me."

The wise woman laughed. "You're talking about *him* again."

"No, I'm not. I'm talking about how *I* feel. *I* feel angry. That's about me."

"Yes, partly," the wise woman said, smiling, "but you're still criticizing *his* behavior. Try speaking without referring to James doing anything wrong."

Carol was speechless, and that's common. Most of us cannot talk about being unhappy without blaming our partners. We've heard other people repeating that pattern all our lives, as in the expression "You make me so mad." In the first place, that belief is wrong—other people *don't* make us angry. In the second place, it's an attitude that ruins our relationships and keeps us stuck—we're handing over the responsibility for changing how *we* feel. In effect we're giving up our ability to choose.

With obvious compassion, the wise woman helped Carol see the *real* cause of her unhappiness: Carol had never felt unconditionally loved. And so, when she married James, she demanded that he make her happy, which he couldn't possibly do because *he* hadn't felt loved, either. When James failed to meet her expectations, Carol felt more empty and afraid than ever. Without any intent to cause harm, she then used all the Getting and Protecting Behaviors with him. She harshly criticized him (attacking) when he didn't give her what she wanted. She whined and complained that he was neglecting her (victim). She never admitted that anything was her fault (lying). And when they had a conversation she couldn't control, she often stomped off into the next room (running).

But because Carol felt accepted and loved by her wise friend, she was able to admit her Getting and Protecting Behaviors and see how they were affecting her marriage. She finally understood that it was the lack of Real Love in her life and *her own* behavior that was causing her unhappiness, not anything her husband was or was not doing.

"Congratulations," said the wise woman. "You just said a lot of true things about yourself, and if you keep doing that, your life will change completely."

"I've been blaming everything on James for years," said Carol, "but now I see that I've been just as awful to him as I thought he was being to me."

"Yes, you have—and without feeling loved, you couldn't have done much better, so there's no reason to feel guilty. Just see the truth about yourself and allow people to accept you with all your flaws. As you feel loved, you'll make much better choices than you have in the past. How do you feel right now?"

"Amazed. I've never talked about my mistakes like this, and it feels very good. You haven't criticized me or looked down on me at all. I like it."

After that single conversation, Carol's entire life gradually began to change. Without exaggeration, Real Love has that effect. She had never before told the truth about her mistakes in that way and been completely accepted by another person. The feeling that follows that experience is indescribable. The Wart King felt it. I have seen it hundreds of times. And it's available to all of us. As we take the bags off our heads and allow people to see who we really are, we create the opportunity for them to accept and love us. And then we can finally feel unconditionally loved, the feeling we want most in all the world. It starts with such a simple act: telling the truth.

The Need for Wise Men and Women— and How to Find Them

The trick, of course, is that we need to be seen, accepted, and loved *while* we're still feeling empty and afraid, and on the occasions when we're angry, wrong, and stupid. That's Real Love, and it's the only kind of love that counts. We need to be seen by people who feel loved enough that they're not blinded by their own needs and fears and can therefore see us clearly and accept us unconditionally. We need people who can stay by our side and help us tell the truth even when we protect ourselves by lying and attacking. We need wise men and women.

Fortunately, we can all find these men and women who will change our lives. We don't need to go to the top of a mountain, as the Wart King did. We don't need to attend expensive seminars run by impressive institutes and listen to motivational speakers. We rarely need professional therapy. Wise men and women are all around us, and to find them we only need to tell the truth about ourselves. Wise men are irresistibly attracted to the truth. *Tell the truth and they will come.*

As you tell the truth about yourself, you will discover that the wise men in your life are your friends, your co-workers, your relatives, your spouse. A wise man can be anyone. Special training and education are not required to produce a wise man—only Real Love is necessary.

But how do you find these people? *Before* you tell someone the truth about yourself, how can you know whether one of your friends is capable of accepting and loving you? *You often can't.* And *that person often doesn't know,* either. There's only one way to know for sure whether someone is truly a wise man—exercise some faith and actually tell the truth about yourself.

As you do that, not only will you *find out* whether the person you're talking to is a wise man—you'll also *help to make* him or her a wise man. As Carol talked to her wise friend, it's true that *Carol* benefited greatly from the Real Love she received. But Carol also gave *her friend* an opportunity to practice being loving. The first time someone shared the truth about herself with Carol's friend, she didn't know she had the ability to be accepting and loving. With time and experience, she developed that ability.

> ✍ As you tell the truth about yourself, you will create opportunities for wise men and women to accept and love you unconditionally.

We all have an inborn desire not only to be loved, but also to love each other, and *if in any given moment we're not empty and afraid,* we will naturally accept and love people who tell the truth about themselves. So, when you tell the truth about yourself, you're giving the people around you an opportunity to find out whether they can be wise men and women, as well as an opportunity for them to develop that natural tendency to accept and love people—in this case, you. As we practice together, we can all become wise men and women, but we won't have that opportunity until one of us has the faith and courage to tell the truth about himself. Wise men are found and created by people who have that kind of faith—people like you.

What do we actually say in order to find these wise men? The words aren't complicated, but they're often different from what we're used to. We talk to people all the time, but we tend to talk about nothing. We talk about the weather, cars, events, and money. We sometimes talk about our feelings, but usually only to complain. For example, we might say that we're angry, but we blame our anger on someone else, which helps no one. We need to learn to talk about the things that will change our lives.

So again, what exactly do we say as we're looking for people who are capable of accepting and loving us? You could say this: "I want to take the bag off my head and tell you the truth about myself. I've never felt unconditionally loved. All my life, I've felt empty, alone, and afraid most of the time. I've tried to fill my emptiness with whatever felt good at the time—praise, power, money, approval, sex, sympathy, things like that. To get those things, I've manipulated people—I've lied, attacked people, and acted like a victim. I've also protected myself from being hurt by lying, attacking people, acting like a victim, and running. Of course, I've never talked about any of this to anyone, because I've been terrified that people would laugh at me or criticize me. But now I want to tell you the truth about myself so that I'll finally be seen for who I really am—so I can really feel accepted and loved."

Fat chance. With experience—and acceptance—you *can* eventually tell the truth about yourself with that kind of boldness, but the above paragraph would be unrealistic for most people in the beginning. It requires too much faith and courage. Most of us need an approach that is less direct and less frightening. If we're uncomfortable telling the truth about ourselves, we won't start. For that reason, I'm going to suggest some ways to tell the truth that have proved successful in the past. I don't propose that any of them is exactly right for you. However, as you read the sample scenarios, you may think of some variations that will be comfortable for you.

Take Responsibility for Your Mistakes. Being accepted when we're "good" means nothing. When people like us only for being beautiful and successful, and for doing what they want, they don't really love *us*. They like how we make *them* feel. We feel loved unconditionally only when we feel accepted by people who see our mistakes and flaws, which is why it's so important that we tell the truth about our imperfections.

When we freely admit our mistakes and see that we're still accepted, we learn that we can be loved even when we're wrong, weak, and foolish. When we feel loved under those conditions, what is there to hide? What is there to fear? That's a great feeling. We all have an innate desire to do the right thing—a conscience—but when we feel unloved, we tend to hide our mistakes and keep on making them. Once we realize we *can* feel loved while admitting our mistakes, it becomes easier to tell the truth about them as we make them, and then we can finally stop making them and choose more wisely. Happily, Caroline and Daniel discovered how this works before their relationship was irreparably damaged.

Caroline had been asking Daniel for three weeks to fix the dripping shower head in the bathroom, and she was irritated when she brought it up again. "That shower head is still dripping, you know. Our water bill is going to go up."

Daniel immediately thought of the usual excuses: "I've been busy. They've been keeping me late at work. I haven't had a chance to work on it." But then he decided to exercise a little faith and tell the truth about himself. So he took a deep breath and said, "I hate to admit it, but I've been putting that job off. Partly, it's a lot of work, but mostly I've put it off because I feel stupid. Nobody ever showed me how to do this kind of stuff, so I usually get in there and make lots of mistakes and then I look dumb. I end up making lots of trips to the hardware store and asking the clerks a bunch of stupid questions. So the truth is that I've had the *time* to do the job, but I've been lazy and feeling stupid. That may not make much sense to you, but there it is."

Caroline lost her anger immediately. She walked over to her husband, hugged him, and they had a wonderful moment of mutual acceptance. And Daniel began to work on the leaky shower head.

We make little mistakes all the time, and then, because we're afraid people won't accept us with them, we hide them in some way. We minimize our mistakes, shift the responsibility for them to other people, or outright lie about them. We've been doing this for so long, we often don't realize we're doing it. You don't need to tell all of the truth about all of your mistakes to everyone. That would be unwise. But you can't begin to experience the rewards of telling the truth about your mistakes until you actually begin to do it. It's well worth it.

Tell the Truth About Yourself as You Talk About People and Events in Your Own Life. We talk to people about what we do all the time. With a little thought and courage, we can turn those moments into extraordinary experiences. Following are some examples of telling the truth.

"I was really irritated with my husband yesterday when he didn't do something I wanted (name the specific thing). And then I realized that I don't have the right to demand that he do everything I want—that's pretty selfish of me, really. And if I'm angry, that's *my* choice, not his fault. All the time we've been married, I've been demanding things from him and expecting him to change, and it's caused a lot of unhappiness. I haven't been accepting him and loving him very much. I've been more interested in my own happiness. I have a lot to learn about relationships."

"My son has had a terrible attitude about a lot of things for some time—school, his chores around the house, the family. And I've been pretty hard on him—restricting him, getting mad at him, stuff like that. Now I'm beginning to believe that the biggest problem in his life is *me*. It's true that he needs to change some things in his life, but he also needs me to love him unconditionally while he learns those things, and I haven't been doing that. All he ever wanted was for me to love him no matter what he did, and I haven't done that. When he screws up, I get irritated at him, and then he can see that I *don't* love him unconditionally. I didn't understand until lately how much that has hurt him. I thought I was a much better father than I really have been."

"Last night my wife did something I didn't like, and I got angry—as usual. But I've been thinking about that. We've been growing farther apart for years, and I always blamed it on her. Now I've come to realize that she's not the problem. I haven't been a very loving husband. I've been selfish and critical—much more concerned about what *I* wanted than what would make *her* happy. I've never admitted that before—it's embarrassing to realize."

"I go to church every Sunday, but I often feel like a real hypocrite. I still get angry at the people around me, and I often don't feel very loving or forgiving. I wonder if I'm a very good example of the things I claim to believe."

"I was lecturing my daughter about something yesterday when I realized that I couldn't remember the last time I just sat with her and told her I loved her. I don't remember my parents ever doing that with me—maybe that's why I don't do it with my daughter. I've always thought of myself as a loving parent, but I think I need to change some things."

"Sometimes I get home from work and realize that I've been way too busy making money and doing *things*. I haven't paid enough attention to my relationships with people and being happy. I need to do something about that. Do you know what I mean?"

Tell the Truth About Yourself as You Talk About People and Events in the Life of Your Partner. In everyday conversation, people tell us a great deal about their lives. When they tell us about their feelings (happiness, sadness, fear, anger), they are telling us how much Real Love they have in their lives. When they tell us about their behavior, they invariably describe their Getting and Protecting Behaviors. On those occasions, you'll have many opportunities to tell the truth about yourself.

Kate wanted to practice telling the truth about herself to someone, but she didn't know how to start. Her friend, Marie, was complaining that her husband, Brian, often spent a lot of time at work and ignored her. But whenever she tried to talk to him about it, he became angry and defensive.

"Brian doesn't sound very happy," suggested Kate.

"No kidding," agreed Marie. "And he makes *my* life pretty miserable, too."

Kate knew it wouldn't do Marie any good to keep complaining about her husband, and she also wanted to share something about herself, so she said, "I've learned that when people aren't happy—like Brian—they just don't feel loved. People want to feel loved more than anything else in the world, and when they don't get that, they try to fill their lives with other things—like success in their careers. That's why he spends so much time at work. And when people don't feel loved, they're also easily frightened—when they're empty, everything seems like a threat. So when Brian gets angry at you, he's really just afraid and trying to get you to quit hurting him."

"How do you know all this?" asked Marie.

"Because I've done all the same things," answered Kate.

Kate then talked about Real Love, Imitation Love, and Getting and Protecting Behaviors. She was also careful to make it clear that she was *not* blaming Marie for Brian's feeling unloved. She explained that he'd felt a lack of Real Love long before he married Marie—although Marie wasn't doing a great job of unconditionally loving him now, either.

As people talk to you about the people and events in their lives, you do need to listen to what they're saying about *themselves,* but you'll also have many opportunities to tell the truth about yourself. Use them.

Notice that as Kate was telling the truth about herself to Marie, she was also being a wise woman for Marie—accepting and loving Marie as she talked about Marie's interaction with Brian. In the process of finding wise men for ourselves, we often have opportunities to be wise men—for moments at a time—for other people. We all learn how to be wise men and women together.

Tell the Truth About Yourself as You Talk About People and Events Unrelated to You and Your Partner. Almost every day most of us have discussions about movies, books, events in the news, and political issues. As we do that, we're talking—without realizing it—about how people are struggling without Real Love, how people are using Imitation Love, and how people are using Getting and Protecting Behaviors. These are great opportunities to tell the truth about *yourself.* For example, we watch many television programs and movies that depict alcohol and drug use. We see celebrities in and out of treatment centers. It's a constant topic of discussion. You could cluck your tongue in wonder and contempt, as most people do, or you could seize the opportunity to tell the truth about your own Getting and Protecting Behaviors. You could say something like this:

"We tend to look down on alcoholics and drug addicts, but these people are just running from the pain in their lives. The greatest need everybody has is to feel unconditionally loved, and when people can't have that, they'll do whatever it takes to numb their pain or fill their emptiness. That's why people use drugs. I haven't used drugs, but there have been many times in my life when I have felt unloved and empty, and I *have* used other things to make myself feel good—money, power, and seeking the approval of other people, for example. Those behaviors are just more socially acceptable than drugs—so people don't look down on me for using them— but they still treat the same problem. I don't know that I'm any better than a drug addict."

This is just *one* example of a Getting and Protecting Behavior. In Chapter Two we talked about many more. For copious examples of Imitation Love and Getting and Protecting Behaviors, open any newspaper or magazine, or turn on the evening news. I guarantee that you'll recognize ways in which your own behaviors are similar to those of everyone else on the planet. The more honest we are, the more opportunities we create to feel loved.

Tell the Truth About How You Feel. All our lives, we were trained by the people around us to hide our feelings, especially our fear and anger. When we quarreled as children, we were told, "Stop that right now!" We were taught that being angry was "bad." And we were taught that being afraid was a sign of weakness. So when we were afraid or angry, most of us learned to hide those feelings. We learned to lie, which resulted in our feeling unloved and alone.

It's important that we be truthful about the times we're afraid and angry. When we interact with other people, we often *wonder* if they will like us. We need to admit that when we *wonder* if someone will like us, we really mean that we're *afraid* he or she might not. We spend most of our lives afflicted with that fear. The *impatience* we experience when people inconvenience us is a form of *anger*. We use a lot of substitute words—*irritated, frustrated, annoyed,* and *bothered*—to hide the fact that what we really are is angry. When we become *offended* by the words or behavior of others, we're both afraid and angry.

If we have not received enough unconditional love, feeling afraid and angry is *unavoidable*. Most of us have those feelings many times every day. When we deny them—even unconsciously—we can't feel seen, accepted, and loved.

Use This Book to Start Talking About Yourself. Here's a sample conversation you might have with a friend.

"I've been reading a book about relationships, and I've been learning some interesting things about people and about myself."

"What have you learned?"

"The book says that people have problems in their relationships because they didn't get enough unconditional love in their lives. The book calls it Real Love."

You might then offer a definition of Real Love and discuss the ways in which you were conditionally loved all your life. Explain what effects conditional love can have and how it has affected you in particular. You might say something like this: "The book says that when people don't feel enough Real Love, they do whatever it takes to fill their emptiness. They fill their lives with Imitation Love—things like praise, power, pleasure, sex, money, sympathy. I've used praise as a form of Imitation Love all my life. I've tried to look good and do things for people so they'd think well of me and say nice things to me. I've used praise like a drug. But it doesn't last. I hide my fears and mistakes, and I end up feeling like people don't see who I really am. So I feel empty and alone a lot of the time. Until I read about it, I didn't realize I was doing all this."

This kind of conversation can be scary, but if you're talking to a wise friend, he or she will accept you with your flaws, and you'll have created an opportunity to be genuinely loved. In addition, your wise friend might tell the truth about himself or herself, and you'll have created an opportunity to be loving yourself.

It's often not easy to turn the spotlight on ourselves—witness the epidemic reluctance of people to raise their hands in class or volunteer for public speaking. However, we're usually more willing to bring up a subject that involves us less directly, such as an athletic event, a political controversy, a movie—or a book. It's for that reason that I suggest using this book as a way to begin telling the truth about yourself. It's a nonthreatening tool for opening the door in conversations with other people.

———

What happens if you tell the truth about yourself in any of the above ways and your partner responds with a blank stare, indicating no interest in you whatever? Remember that you're not trying to *make* this person love you; you're trying to *find out* if this particular person is capable of being a wise man in that moment, and in this case the answer is *no*. You haven't lost a thing. You simply change the subject back to football or the weather or shopping.

But don't stop there. Keep trying the same conversation with other friends, and eventually you *will* find someone whose eyes light up when you talk about who you really are. You *will* find someone—likely several people—who will say something like "Wow! That was honest." You will find someone who is attracted to the truth and who will accept you as you are. And that person will likely share the truth about himself, too. That's how you find wise men. They're everywhere, and most of them don't even know who they are. When you finally get that warm feeling of unconditional acceptance from one person, you won't care one bit how many puzzled expressions you got from others before that. Real Love is worth everything we invest to find it. Everything!

When you do find someone who accepts a little bit of the truth about you, tell him or her a little more. With each dose of acceptance, your confidence will grow, and you'll find it easier to share even more about yourself. You may not want to dump all your problems on any one person all at once. These wise men are not therapists, just loving friends. If you feel that you're overwhelming someone, back off a step and try again later—but more slowly.

Remember that it doesn't matter how many people *don't* accept and love you. It only matters that there are some people who *do*, and you'll never find those people if you don't allow them to see who you are. I know it can seem frightening to tell the truth about yourself—because people *might not* like you—but the alternative is to lie about who you are, which *guarantees* that you'll feel unloved and alone, the worst condition of all. You really have nothing to lose by taking the bag off your head.

Feeling seen and loved by just one person can change our lives completely, but when we associate with more than one wise man or woman, we multiply the likelihood of getting that feeling. For this reason, many people meet in small groups with the conscious intent of telling the truth about themselves and loving each other. It's not therapy, it doesn't cost anything, and no formal membership is required. These are just "regular people," and the results of their conversations are life changing.

A Few Words of Caution

Don't expect that any one person will be able to love you unconditionally all the time. That's almost impossible, but luckily it also isn't necessary, because feeling accepted even for moments has a miraculous effect, and as those moments grow longer and more frequent, the effect becomes more powerful.

Also, in the process of telling the truth about yourself, never forget the Law of Expectations, which we discussed in Chapter Three. As soon as you *expect* any one person to accept and love you, you will ruin the possibility of feeling unconditionally loved. Real Love is *freely* given and received. Expectations ruin the possibility of feeling Real Love. You will change your relationships and your happiness dramatically if you can just stop insisting that any one person accept or love you. *Simply tell the truth about yourself and wait to be loved by whoever is capable of loving you unconditionally.* When you can exercise the faith to take that approach, you create the opportunity to feel unconditionally loved.

A wonderful sense of freedom comes from telling the truth about ourselves. Even when our partners fail to accept us, telling the truth allows *us* to shrug off the enormous burden of lies that keeps us alone and unhappy. However, it's still not wise to tell the truth about ourselves to everyone, and we need to identify the occasions when it could be harmful.

Most of the time, we can't know whether telling the truth

about ourselves is unwise until we've actually done it. If you're sharing yourself with someone and that person is clearly not accepting you, and that feels painful, simply stop. Or if the person you're speaking with seems to feel threatened or in some way excessively responsible for your feelings when you express your fear or anger, stop. If a person doesn't feel loved himself, listening to you express your feelings can be overwhelming. For that reason, you need to be sensitive about continuing to express your feelings when people are being injured by them.

In some situations, we can judge *before* speaking that telling the truth about ourselves might be harmful to others. For example, when we understand that our emptiness and fear started in childhood, we may be tempted to share that insight with our parents. But most parents feel threatened by any discussion of their mistakes. To insist that they participate in such a conversation would be unloving on our part.

On still other occasions, we can know before speaking that telling the truth about ourselves would be unnecessarily harmful *to us*. If our employer and co-workers knew everything about our fears and flaws, our careers could be affected in an *unnecessarily* negative way. We do need to be truthful about ourselves, but we don't have to do it with the people at work, where the risks are needlessly multiplied.

The Rules of Seeing

Many of us have lied for so long that we really don't know how to be truthful about ourselves. And we've spent so much time telling others what they've done to us or failed to do for us, that we don't really know how to *see* another person who is trying to be truthful about himself. Being honest can seem strange and uncomfortable, like learning a foreign language.

The following rules or guidelines make it easier for us to see each other.

I will refer to anyone who is speaking or communicating nonverbally (smiling, crying, withdrawing, sulking) as the *speaker*. The speaker is heard and seen by one or more *listeners*.

The First Rule of Seeing: "One speaker." During any truly productive interaction, there can only be one speaker. When two or more people compete to speak, no one is completely heard or seen.

The Second Rule of Seeing: "Whoever speaks first is the speaker." Everyone else listens. This doesn't prevent anyone else from speaking. It simply determines the order of speaking and ensures that everyone will be heard.

Sarah and Kevin often argued, and on this occasion Sarah was especially annoyed. "You're always sulking and snapping at me and the kids, and I'm tired of it. I get home from work and need some help around here, and all I get from you is growling and complaining."

"I wouldn't snap at you if you ever did what I asked you to do," Kevin responded. "How many times have I asked you for those receipts so I could file our income tax?"

We all know where the conversation went from there. They exchanged accusations and added even more wounds to their damaged relationship. That always happens when two people try to be heard at the same time. Kevin and Sarah were talking about two separate subjects, and neither was listening to the other.

They invited a wise friend to help them talk to each other. After he explained the Rules of Seeing, Sarah spoke. "Like I said, I really hate it when you're grouchy at me and the kids. I have a lot to do, and I need your help, not your biting my head off."

Kevin responded as usual to this old attack. "I still don't have those receipts I need for the income tax. I need your help, too, you know."

"Kevin," the wise man said, "Sarah spoke first, so let's try letting her finish before we talk about another subject, like the receipts you need. It really does work better that way—those are the first two Rules of Seeing that we talked about."

Kevin, however, was eager to pursue the subject he had introduced. "But she—"

"Think about it," said the wise man. "In all these years, have the two of you ever had a productive, loving conversation when you both tried to talk at the same time?"

"Well . . ."

"Even once?"

Kevin let out a long sigh. "I guess not."

"So you've already *proven* that when you both talk at the same time, both of you lose. Do you want to keep doing something that never works, or would you be willing to try something different? If you want to do things this new way, you can still talk about Sarah all you want, but not right now."

"Okay, I'll wait till she's done before I talk," said Kevin.

"If you plan on talking about her as soon as she's finished, you'll be thinking about what you're going to say instead of really listening to her, and she won't feel like you listened to her. I suggest you talk about the income tax receipts tomorrow or even later."

Kevin had always defended himself when he felt threatened. That made him feel safer for a moment, but when he did that, Sarah felt ignored and unloved, and Kevin felt more alone—consistently terrible consequences for both of them.

After he understood that he'd have the chance to speak later—and because he trusted his wise friend—Kevin chose to listen, which created a new and delightful experience for both him and Sarah. Sarah got to express herself completely without being interrupted or attacked. She felt seen and understood by Kevin. And he learned things about her that he'd never known. None of that could have happened if they'd both insisted on talking at the same time.

The one exception to the First and Second Rules of Seeing occurs when two people feel sufficiently loved and loving that they can speak *and* listen to each other at the same time. In that case, there are two speakers and two listeners in the conversation. Before you make an exception to the rules, however, be certain that both you and your partner are capable of listening to each other, and that you are not *competing* to be the speaker.

The Third Rule of Seeing: "The speaker describes himself." Almost every time someone speaks, he's saying something important about *himself.*

When Sarah said Kevin snapped at her, it would have been a useless distraction to talk about *Kevin*—why he snapped, how often he snapped, or what he said. The real message Sarah was trying to communicate was that *she* felt unloved, frightened, and alone.

While Sarah talked, the wise man listened intently and occasionally helped her to express her feelings of fear and loneliness instead of getting lost in the details of past conflicts with Kevin. Even though many of her initial words involved Kevin, the discussion was really about *her,* not him.

As Sarah felt the acceptance and love of the wise man, her anger evaporated. Kevin had never seen her calm down so quickly. Getting angry at her had certainly never accomplished that. The pain of emptiness and fear is overwhelming. In that condition, our thoughts and actions are all centered around protecting ourselves and filling our own needs. A wise man knows that, and as he accepts and loves the speaker, that person finally gets what he needs—Real Love. That eliminates the emptiness and fear that are always the real problem in any relationship.

The Fourth Rule of Seeing: "If you can't be a wise man, get one." Whenever our partners speak to us, they need someone capable of seeing them clearly and accepting them. When we're empty and afraid ourselves, we're blind to anything but our own needs and fears, and that makes a productive conversation with any partner nearly impossible. As a wise man accepts and loves us, we can often feel safe enough to stop protecting ourselves and tell the truth about ourselves. As we continue to feel loved, we can acquire the ability to see our partners clearly and accept them. When we feel nervous, afraid, irritated, or impatient as we're talking to someone, we need to stop repeating our ineffective feelings and behaviors and reach out to feel the love of a wise man or woman.

Kevin and Sarah had tried to communicate with each other on countless occasions, but they failed because neither

 The Four Rules of Seeing

1. One speaker at a time
2. Whoever speaks first is the speaker
3. The speaker describes only him or herself
4. If you can't be a wise man, get one

of them felt loved enough to see and accept the other. They were too blinded by their individual needs and fears. When they finally realized they couldn't function as wise men for each other, they decided to try the Fourth Rule of Seeing—they called their wise friend, who helped them both feel accepted and loved enough that they could begin to see and accept each other.

The story of Kevin and Sarah is true, but it describes an ideal situation. Let's be practical—in many relationships it just wouldn't work if you asked a wise man to join a conversation between you and your partner. In those situations, I suggest that you modify the Fourth Rule slightly: *"If you need a wise man, get one (at least for yourself)."* Janet illustrates the application of that rule in the following story.

In the department where she worked, a new supervisor took over and began making changes that required more work and flexibility from Janet. She felt threatened by the changes and reacted by marching into his office and having an angry conversation with him. At the end of the day, she called a wise friend and said, "This guy is horrible. He doesn't know anything, but he's already changing my hours and my job description. I'm mad about it."

Her wise friend calmly said, "You're afraid."

That was not the response Janet had expected.

"What are you talking about?" she asked.

Her friend replied, "Every time we're angry, we're really just protecting ourselves from something we're afraid of. You're afraid of your new boss, and you're using anger to protect yourself."

The wise woman helped Janet see that when the new supervisor ordered her to do things differently, she felt as if her opinion didn't matter—which she interpreted as another confirmation that nobody cared about her. She was also afraid she'd make mistakes and be criticized. In short, she was afraid that, in this new situation, neither her new supervisor nor her co-workers would respect or like her. *Our anger is a reaction to fear, and our fear is almost always about not feeling loved.*

The wise woman continued. "You get angry because then you feel less powerless. In addition, you know that if you act irritated and intimidating, your new supervisor might not ask you to do some of the things you don't want to do. I'm not suggesting that you do any of this intentionally, but no matter *why* you do it, it will never make you happy. You've already proven that a million times over."

"That's true," Janet said. "So what do I do when I feel angry with this man? It doesn't help to tell him I'm mad, so should I just keep it to myself and pretend I'm not angry?"

"No, lying about your anger won't help, either. You do need to be truthful, *but not with him.* When you're angry, share your feelings with someone who can love you while you feel that way—and who can keep you honest."

The next time Janet was angry at work, she stopped talking and said, "I'll be right back. I have to make a phone call." Then she went into another room and called her wise friend. "I'm mad at him again. I want to slap him—he's so stupid."

"What are you afraid of?" her friend asked.

Janet immediately smiled as she realized, once more, that the true cause of her anger was not her boss. She was just afraid of being criticized and not loved. When she saw that, and when she felt loved by her friend, her fear disappeared, along with her anger. In this case, Janet didn't need to be a wise man for her boss, nor did she need a wise man to come in and mediate a conversation between her and her boss. She just needed *someone* to see, accept, and love her.

People all over the country are learning to reach out, tell

the truth about themselves, and get loved instead of wallowing in their fear and anger, and they're experiencing dramatic changes in their happiness. Being loved is the most powerful force on the planet.

> Every time we're angry, we're really just protecting ourselves from something we're afraid of. Usually the thing we're afraid of is not feeling loved.

Exercises in Truth-Telling

In the course of everyday life, we can learn how to tell the truth about ourselves, feel loved, and love others. But we can also accelerate that process by participating in exercises that provide opportunities to be loved and to love others. Once you've found people who are interested in hearing and telling the truth, I suggest using the following exercises. Each exercise can be repeated many times. The more often you do an exercise, the more you can learn from it.

I'll be describing these exercises as if there were two people participating, but they can be done by any number of participants. I suggest several guidelines to be considered when doing the exercises:

1. There is one speaker and one listener. That is the First Rule of Seeing, which we discussed in the previous section. The listener may ask an *occasional* question to clarify what the speaker is saying, but on the whole, the listener *listens*. The listener does not offer comments about what the speaker is saying, nor does the listener talk about himself.
2. After the speaker has finished, he becomes the listener and the listener becomes the new speaker. It's important that

the new speaker not use this opportunity to comment on what the original speaker said.

3. After both participants have had the opportunity to be the speaker, they talk about what they learned—mostly about themselves, but also what they learned about their partner. This part of the exercise is not intended for lecturing, arguing, debating, or contradicting what any speaker has said. For a few examples of what some participants have learned when they've done these exercises, see the "Lessons" section following each exercise.

———

Most people communicate more openly with one or two people than they do in a large group. For that reason, when the exercises are done in groups, I suggest that the group be broken up into pairs. When everyone has had the opportunity to be a speaker, the entire group can then reassemble and discuss what each person learned. That way, everyone can learn from the experiences of all the people in the group.

In groups containing odd numbers of people, there will obviously be one group of three. In that group, there will be one speaker and two listeners for each interaction, and therefore it may take a bit longer to complete the exercise.

Exercise 1: Telling the Truth About Ourselves

For one or two minutes, the first speaker tells the truth about himself and the listener listens. The listener then becomes the speaker and repeats the exercise. Both participants then talk about what they've learned from speaking and from listening.

COMMENT

When we hide the truth about ourselves, we feel alone and can't have loving relationships with anyone. Truth-telling creates the possibility of being seen, accepted, and loved. It's especially effective to talk about our mistakes and flaws, because, obviously, we feel most unconditionally loved when we're accepted with our mistakes, not our successes.

We have a tendency in this exercise—as elsewhere—to talk about *things* rather than ourselves. We talk about our jobs, our houses, our children, and so on. But if we want to feel seen and accepted, we must eventually learn to share the truth about who *we* really are, warts and all. Following are some examples of telling the truth about ourselves:

"I feel uncomfortable doing this exercise. It's not easy for me to talk about myself."

"I'm not as happy as I want to be. I guess that's why I'm here talking to you now."

"Not many people know I take an antidepressant. I've been doing that for over a year."

"I sometimes drink more than I should."

"I've been pretty selfish all my life. What *I* want has always been more important to me than what other people want."

"Telling you the truth makes me nervous, so it's obvious that I don't do it very much. I tend to hide who I really am."

"I've always been ashamed about how short I am."

"I have not been a loving husband. I yell at my wife and usually ignore what she wants."

"I feel alone and afraid most of the time."

"I worry a lot about what people think of me."

"I'm embarrassed about being overweight."

"I've been through some lousy relationships with men (or women)."

"I wish I had more friends than I do."

LESSONS

"I felt afraid while I was telling you the truth about myself, but it got easier the more I did it. It's a relief to be myself with someone and stop hiding for a change."

"After I told you the truth about myself, I felt less alone."

"When you talked about yourself, I felt closer to you. I didn't care about the mistakes you'd made in your life. In fact, I care more about you now than I did before."

"I felt like you were really listening to me as I talked about myself, and I liked that. I haven't had many experiences like this."

"I'm amazed at how much I've learned about you in these few minutes. I know more about you than I do about most of the friends I've had for years."

"As I talked to you, I realized how little anybody knows about me. You know more about who I really am after a few minutes than most people I've known for years."

"As you talked about the mistakes you've made, it was a lot easier for me to talk about mine. I'm glad you were the speaker first."

Exercise 2: Fear

For one or two minutes, the speaker tells the listener about his fears. The listener then becomes the speaker and talks about his fears. And then they both discuss what they've learned.

COMMENT

The more we tell the truth about ourselves, the more opportunities we create to be seen and accepted. We feel most loved when we feel accepted with the qualities we're ashamed of— such as our fears. When we can talk about our fears and feel accepted, we lose our reason to be afraid. Following are some examples of fears we might share:

"I've always been afraid that if people really got to know me, they'd laugh at me and think I was stupid. I'm afraid right now that you'll learn too much about me and not like me."
"I'm afraid of losing my job."
"I really hate how my marriage is now, and I'm afraid it will never get any better."
"When I was a kid, I never raised my hand to answer a question in class, because I was afraid somebody would laugh at me. I'm still afraid to talk around people for the same reason."
"There are times when I drink to make my fears go away."
"I'm afraid my children don't love me."
"I'm afraid to admit that I don't know nearly as much as I've always pretended I do."
"I'm afraid to tell you what I'm really thinking, because you'll think I'm crazy."
"I'm afraid of dying."

LESSONS

"What a relief that was! I've never talked about being afraid before."
"As you talked about your fears, I felt closer to you. And that helps me to believe that my own fears might not be completely disgusting to other people."
"After this, I think it will be easier to tell the truth about myself again."
"I felt accepted by you when I described my fears. I feel less anxious and alone right now."
"I never realized how afraid I am—of many things."

Exercise 3: Telling the Truth About How We Get and Protect

For one or two minutes, the speaker describes his Getting and Protecting Behaviors to the listener. The listener then becomes the speaker. And then they discuss what they've learned.

COMMENTS

The "bad" things we do are just behaviors intended to protect ourselves and get Imitation Love. This exercise requires more thought than the simple truth-telling of Exercises 1 and 2. I therefore recommend that you do two things before beginning Exercise 3:

1. Review the principles found in Chapter Four.
2. If possible, have someone present who is experienced in identifying Getting and Protecting Behaviors—in other words, a wise man.

Following are some examples of things a speaker might say:

"When people criticize me, I protect myself by *attacking* them, usually with anger. I've done that more times than I can count."

"I'm always afraid of making mistakes and being laughed at, so I tend to avoid people. That's *running*."

"I'm beginning to realize that I complain a lot. When I complain that things aren't fair and that people don't treat me right, I'm trying to get people to sympathize with me. When I do that, I'm acting like a *victim,* and I do that pretty often."

"I talk about the good things I do so that people will be impressed and like me. But of course I don't tell them I'm trying to get them to like me, so that's *lying*."

"I tend to hide my mistakes and blame them on other people, because I'm afraid of looking bad. I'm *lying*."

"I get angry at my kids a lot, and then I blame it on them. But now I'm understanding that my anger is not their fault. I just feel empty and afraid about things that have nothing to do with them. I *attack* my kids with anger, because then I briefly feel less powerless and alone."

Without interrupting the speaker too often, it's occasionally helpful to encourage him to provide specific examples of the things he says. When a speaker says he gets angry at people, ask him to give an example from the last couple of days. Doing that allows him to feel even more seen and accepted.

LESSONS

"I didn't realize until today how much I manipulate people to like me. And it doesn't work anyway. It only feels good for a short time, and what I get doesn't really make me feel loved or happy."

"As we talk, I'm realizing that when I protect myself, I always feel alone. Being truthful with you has felt much better than protecting myself from you would have."

"As I listen to you talk about protecting yourself, I begin to see that when other people are angry at me, they're not really trying to hurt me—they're just protecting themselves. Knowing that makes me realize it's stupid for me to get angry at them."

"I've been using Getting and Protecting Behaviors from the time I was a small child, and I can see they've caused me a lot of unhappiness. I'd like to give them up and try telling the truth about myself instead."

Exercise 4: Telling the Truth About the Lies We Tell

For one or two minutes, the speaker describes some of the common, everyday lies he tells, along with what he's learned about those lies. The listener then becomes the speaker. And then they discuss what they've learned.

COMMENTS

Without meaning to, most of tell many lies in a day. As we tell the truth about them with each other, we're better able to see them, feel loved, and stop telling them. Following are a few examples of the lies we tell:

"Sometimes when my wife asks me about something I promised to do, and I didn't do it, I say 'I forgot,' but that's not quite true. What happens is that I just don't *want* to do what she asks me to do, so I *choose* to put it so far down on my list of priorities that I neglect it intentionally, or eventually I really do forget about it. I don't forget the things I *want* to remember—I never forget to watch the Super Bowl."

"I blame my husband for making me angry all the time. I may not come right out and say it, but I know I communicate it to him in many ways—and he feels it. When I do that, I'm also saying he doesn't have a right to make choices that inconvenience me. And those are both huge lies. Nobody is responsible for my anger but me. It's my choice."

"I sometimes say 'I'm sorry' to people when I don't really mean it. I just say it so they won't be even angrier than they are. If I were really sorry, I wouldn't have done what I did in the first place. What I really mean is that I'm sorry I got caught and looked foolish."

"I've told a few friends that I'm just not in love with my wife anymore. As much as I hate to see it, the truth is that I'm just selfish. I want her to make *me* happy, and when she doesn't do that, I say I don't love her. I have a lot to learn about caring for *her* happiness."

LESSONS

"Now that I've told the truth about my lies, I don't feel as likely to tell those same lies again."

"I'm going to go home and tell my husband I've been wrong all these years to blame him for my anger."

"After hearing what you said about 'I forgot' and 'I'm sorry,' I can see I've been using the same lies. You've helped me to be more honest."

Giving Up the Getting and Protecting Behaviors

Every moment of our lives, we make choices. And then we experience the consequences, which we do not get to choose. When we choose wisely, we're happy; when we don't, we're not. It's really that simple. The consequences of choosing Getting and Protecting Behaviors are always Imitation Love, emptiness, and fear—never Real Love or genuine happiness.

Years ago, a man came to my medical office complaining of a headache he'd had for several months. A radiologic scan of his head revealed a large brain tumor. I asked him why he'd waited so long before coming to see me and he said, "I don't know. I guess it didn't hurt that much."

I could see from the expression on his wife's face that he'd been experiencing more pain than he was admitting, so I asked him if he'd been taking anything for pain.

"I've had some whiskey now and then," he responded.

After more questions, I learned that he'd been drinking increasing quantities of alcohol to eliminate his pain, and he only came to see me when more than a quart of whiskey per day failed to give him adequate relief. By that time, however, the tumor had become too large to treat. This man died because he'd treated his *pain* instead of treating the *cause* of the pain. Similarly, when we use Getting and Protecting Behaviors—and the Imitation Love we obtain with these behaviors—we treat our pain instead of addressing the real problem, which is the lack of unconditional love in our lives. The result is deadly, as was the case with my patient. While we're using Getting and Protecting Behaviors—while we're enjoying the flow of praise, power, pleasure, and safety that these behaviors give us—we feel a temporary and superficial satisfaction that we confuse with genuine happiness. And then we see no reason to tell the truth about ourselves and pursue the path that leads to Real Love.

In short, Getting and Protecting Behaviors delay our pursuit of Real Love, which in turn prevents us from being happy—our entire reason for existence. That is no small matter. And in addition to distracting us from our pursuit of Real Love, these behaviors prevent us from *feeling* Real Love even when it's offered to us.

As we feel more unconditionally loved, we *naturally* lose our need to use Getting and Protecting Behaviors. However, simply waiting for those behaviors to gradually disappear can sometimes take a long time. In light of their terribly destructive effect, we need to make a *conscious effort* to give up our Getting and Protecting Behaviors, and not just wait for them to go away.

Few of us are eager to do that, however, because we've used them since childhood to get the only kind of "happiness" we've ever known. Imitation Love feels good temporarily, and in the absence of Real Love, we're understandably reluctant to relinquish our enjoyment of praise, power, pleasure, and safety. Elaine and Susan illustrate the benefits of making a conscious choice to give up our Getting and Protecting Behaviors.

Elaine had never felt loved unconditionally. Empty and afraid, she constantly manipulated people and protected herself. She attacked the people who dared to criticize her, and she clung tightly to those who gave her any attention. Predictably, with all those Getting and Protecting Behaviors, she never found Real Love, and her relationships were frustrating and unsatisfying.

Elaine had a wise friend who tried to help her see the truth about her selfishness and her Getting and Protecting Behaviors so she would feel accepted and loved for who she really was and could begin to make wiser choices in her life and in her relationships. But Elaine chose to talk about how badly her husband and other people treated her. In other words, she *lied* about her own behavior, *attacked* her husband and others, and acted like a *victim*—all Getting and Protecting Behaviors. She was given many opportunities to tell the truth about herself, but instead she tried to manipulate her friend for praise and sympathy. Her friend introduced her to other wise men and women, but Elaine tried to manipulate them, too. Because of that, she was unable to feel the Real Love she was being offered, and she remained empty and frustrated. Eventually, feeling as miserable and alone as ever, she simply stopped associating with these people who were trying to love her. By doing that, she was using yet another Protecting Behavior—running.

Like Elaine, Susan was also empty, afraid, and unhappy. She associated with the same group of wise men and women

Elaine had known. But unlike Elaine, Susan decided to exercise faith in the ability of people to love her as she told the truth about herself—without manipulating them. They helped her identify the times she lied, attacked people, and acted like a victim—and she listened. That made it possible for her to *feel* the Real Love she was being offered, the same love that Elaine could not feel because of her refusal to tell the truth about herself. Feeling a kind of love and happiness she'd never known, Susan no longer had a reason to use her Getting and Protecting Behaviors and was increasingly able to give them up.

But Susan didn't lose her Getting and Protecting Behaviors just because she felt more loved. She also lost them because she'd made a *conscious choice*—based on faith and courage—to trust other people and to stop lying, attacking people, running, and acting like a victim. Any time we decide to tell other people the truth about ourselves, we're making a decision to stop using our Getting and Protecting Behaviors, and we greatly accelerate our ability to feel Real Love. It's a wise decision we're all capable of making.

As many people contemplate telling the truth about themselves and giving up their Getting and Protecting Behaviors, they say, "I don't think I can do this. It's just too hard." On the contrary. Telling the truth is far easier than the complicated and never-ending effort of lying, getting angry, acting like a victim, and otherwise protecting ourselves in order to get Imitation Love. Telling the truth about ourselves doesn't require nearly as much effort as using Getting and Protecting Behaviors. It just takes more faith.

What I've been suggesting here is that we would feel more loved if we simply exercised more *self-control* and stopped using our destructive Getting and Protecting Behaviors. On the other hand, I've previously stated that in the absence of Real Love, we are empty and afraid, and in that condition we *will* use Getting and Protecting Behaviors. So how can I now suggest that we simply *stop* them if we don't feel loved? Don't we have to find Real Love *before* we can stop using our Getting and Protecting Behaviors? No, not entirely. We can engage in both efforts at the same time, and the two complement each other.

We human beings do have a unique capacity to make self-determined decisions. It's true that in the absence of Real Love, our ability to make wise and loving decisions *is* impaired—sometimes severely—but we can still choose to limit our Getting and Protecting Behaviors *to some degree.* The more we can exercise our self-control and restrain our natural tendency to use Getting and Protecting Behaviors, the easier it will be for us to feel unconditionally loved and loving. Susan and Elaine proved that. And the more we tell the truth about ourselves and find Real Love, the less need we'll have to use Getting and Protecting Behaviors.

Self-control and Real Love have a powerful synergy. If we really want to change our lives and be happy, we can't just sit back and wait to feel more loved. Nor can we merely grip life by the horns and attempt to take complete control. We need to take every advantage of both approaches simultaneously.

> As we feel unconditionally loved, we lose our need to use Getting and Protecting Behaviors. If, in addition, we simultaneously exercise self-control over our Getting and Protecting Behaviors, we can greatly accelerate our feelings of unconditional love.

Most of us don't have much experience exercising faith, telling the truth about ourselves, and feeling Real Love. For that reason, the first few times we attempt to give up the Getting and Protecting Behaviors we've used all our lives can be frightening. Between the time we give up Imitation Love and the time we feel Real Love—the "in-between time"—we may feel as though we have no source of happiness at all. When we feel afraid and don't yet feel loved, we tend to reach out for the familiar and predictable satisfaction of Imitation Love.

But as we keep taking the other steps to finding love (desire to change, exercising faith, telling the truth), we'll significantly shorten the "in-between" time and will not feel lost and afraid as we let go of the Getting and Protecting Behaviors. The more often we tell the truth about ourselves, for example, to people capable of seeing and loving us, the sooner we feel seen, accepted, and loved. And then we won't feel the temptation to reach out for the old tools of getting and protecting.

When we believe the world to be unloving and harsh, we naturally see evidence everywhere to support our belief. We even see attacks where there are none and have a tendency to protect ourselves. But when we simply *choose* to have faith in the possibility of being loved—as Susan did—we see the evidence that people accept and love us much faster, and the "in-between" time becomes much shorter.

5

The Effect of Real Love

Like Money in the Bank

As we feel unconditionally loved, we lose our emptiness and fear, and then we no longer have a *need* for Getting and Protecting Behaviors. When we stop lying, being angry, attacking people, acting like victims, and running, our relationships can only become more loving and rewarding. Let me illustrate how Real Love affects our lives simply by eliminating our anger.

Real Love Is Like Money in the Bank

Imagine that you're down to your last two dollars, and you're hungry. Putting the money on a table, you get ready to go out and buy some bread. Suddenly, I dash into the room, snatch the two dollars off the table, and run away before you can stop me. You'd almost certainly be angry at me.

Now imagine that I do exactly the same thing—steal two dollars off your table as you get ready to go out and buy some bread—but this time you know you have twenty *million* dollars in the bank. How would you feel this time? The loss of two dollars matters very little when you have twenty million.

That's how it feels to have sufficient Real Love. It's like having twenty million dollars all the time. And then, when people are inconsiderate, when they fail to do what we want, and even when they attack us, they're only taking two dollars, which we can easily afford to lose. When we feel unconditionally loved, everything else becomes relatively insignificant. People don't "make" us angry anymore. Heavy traffic, for example, becomes a tiny nuisance, not something that makes us angry and unhappy, as it once did. When people speak badly of us, we're not threatened; we understand that they're simply afraid and protecting themselves. The wounds of the past begin to heal and no longer cast their terrible shadow over everything we do in the present. Mark illustrates this effect of Real Love.

Mark and his wife had always traded Imitation Love in the form of approval, praise, attention, and sex. Remember that those things are not inherently bad, and become forms of Imitation Love only when they're used as substitutes for Real Love. In the beginning, Mark and his wife were content with that—it was the only kind of "happiness" they'd ever known. But after a year of marriage, as the thrill of Imitation Love wore off, they both became increasingly dissatisfied with their relationship. Mark talked to a wise friend who suggested that he would benefit from telling the truth about himself, especially about his mistakes, but Mark said, "I don't understand how talking about my mistakes will make me happy."

"You'll never *understand* it," said his friend, "until you *experience* it, and that takes faith. You can only feel loved and happy *after* you actually tell the truth about yourself, and that requires faith on your part. What have you got to lose? How can it hurt to try something different? Do you like the way your life is going now?"

Mark smiled as he mumbled, "No."

Mark began to tell the truth about himself to his friend and to a few other loving men and women who helped him see how often he lied, attacked people, acted like a victim, and ran from relationships. Mark felt accepted by these people as he took the bag off his head and allowed them to see who he really was, warts and all. One day he phoned his friend and said, "I just had an amazing conversation with my wife."

"What happened?" his friend asked.

"She was furious with me for something I promised to do and then forgot about. When she does that, I usually get angry, too, and everything just goes downhill from there. But this time it was different. Because of the conversations I've been having with you and some other people, I remembered that there were people who cared about me. So when she got angry at me, I didn't get upset."

"It makes quite a difference to feel loved, doesn't it?" asked the wise man.

"It makes a big difference," Mark agreed. "Because I felt loved by you and the others, there was nothing to be upset about. This is great."

"What did you say to her?" asked the wise man.

"I put my arms around her and told her I'd been thoughtless and selfish, not only then but on many occasions. You wouldn't believe what she did then: she cried. It was incredible. I wish I'd done this a long time ago."

"You couldn't have. You didn't feel loved enough to do it before now."

That is the effect of Real Love. When we exercise faith and tell the truth about ourselves, we begin to feel the love that banishes emptiness and fear. We can then choose to climb out of the bottomless pit we've dug for ourselves with our Getting and Protecting Behaviors.

> Sufficient Real Love is like having twenty million dollars all the time. Then, when other people are uncooperative or unkind, it's like they're taking two dollars we don't miss.

The Effect of Real Love on the Past and Present

For most of us, the past and present are inseparably intertwined, and understandably so. The way we've been treated by a particular group of people in the past can have an enormous impact not only on how we see *that group* in the present and the future, but also on how we see *everyone else*. For example, when we were young, our parents and a few others played a very large role in determining our view of the entire world, and if we didn't receive sufficient Real Love from them—I offer no *blaming* here, only an *understanding*—we learned to react to everyone else with Getting and Protecting Behaviors, usually for the rest of our lives.

This explains why Mark usually responded to his wife's anger with his own anger. Because he'd received insufficient Real Love as a child, he felt unloved, empty, and afraid long before he met his wife. When she confronted him with anger, he was already in pain as the result of a lifetime of emptiness and fear, and he immediately reacted to both *her* anger in the present (which told him he wasn't loved) and *his* entire lifetime of emptiness and fear (which carried the same painful message) with the predominant Protecting Behavior he'd been using for decades—his own anger.

But on the occasion Mark described to his friend, he'd felt enough Real Love that he wasn't affected by the lack of unconditional love from his childhood. Without that chronic, debilitating burden of emptiness and fear from the past, he wasn't frightened by his wife's anger in the present, so it didn't become the straw that broke the camel's back—instead, it rolled off his back like water off a duck. Sufficient Real Love eliminates our emptiness and fear from both the past and the present.

Other people's anger disturbs us only because we feel unloved when they get angry. But the solution is not to control their anger, or attack them in return, or run, or act like a victim. Once we start using the Getting and Protecting Behaviors, the exhausting efforts never stop, and we're never happy. The solution is to feel loved, and we don't need to feel loved by everyone. We don't need to feel loved by the people from our past who once failed to love us. We just need to know that *we are loved by someone.*

> When you feel Real Love from just *one* person, that love gives you greater strength to interact with *everyone* else in your life.

Most of us carry around the present and cumulative effects of many wounds. We've experienced uncounted broken promises, unkind words, and moments when our hopes for acceptance have been brutally crushed. Some of us have experienced more overt abuse and infidelity. How do we live with that pain? It helps enormously when we remember—as we discussed in Chapters One and Two—that other people hurt us only because they themselves are drowning and doing what it takes to protect themselves and fill their own emptiness. When we can remember that, we don't take our injuries so personally. I realize that still leaves us painfully empty and alone, but it allows us to see that all our wounds really come from only one source—that we don't feel loved. Fortunately, the solution then becomes clear. We no longer need to exact justice from the individual people who have hurt us, nor to obsess over each injury. We just need to take the steps to find Real Love from those who have it to give. The healing effect is universal: As we feel loved by anyone, we begin to heal all our wounds.

You may still be asking, what do we do about those people who may *still* be hurting us? You certainly can't control their behavior. As you fill your life with Real Love, it really is like putting money in the bank, and eventually, when you feel sufficiently loved, it's like having twenty million dollars. When people do offensive things, those things just don't seem as hurtful as they once did. However, you are still not obligated to allow someone to take money off your table whenever he or she wants to. You can choose to end a relationship when you wish, and we'll talk about that more in Chapter Nine.

Real Love can heal even the most traumatic wounds from the past. As a young teenager, Nicole had been sexually abused on multiple occasions by her older brother and stepfather. When I met her, she was in her mid-thirties, and she was miserable. She'd been in therapy for years and had analyzed each abusive episode with her therapist in great detail. She'd attended sexual-abuse support groups and talked about her abuse to many people. But all her therapy and support had only served to make her feel like a victim. She was completely incapable of a relationship with a man and had no healthy relationships with women. Her life was filled with her own anger and the anger and sympathy of others, which temporarily gave her some emotional relief from her sense of complete emptiness. But she had to work very hard to get these forms of Imitation Love, and because she still had no peaceful, unconditional love in her life, she still was not happy.

People who have been abused don't just act *like* victims—they really *are* victims. It's only *natural* that when we've been injured by the aggression and perversion of others, we feel hurt and angry, but unfortunately, if we continue to indulge in what's *natural,* we simply can't be happy. As we feel like victims, we feel weak and helpless, and when we act like victims, that Getting and Protecting Behavior keeps us from feeling the Real Love we really need to heal our lives and be happy.

I am not saying that victims don't need to talk about their pain, or that they don't need sympathy for their pain. They do. But victims need to avoid making their wounds the focus of their lives. Their wounds are a part of who they are—but only *one* part, not the definition of who they are. They also need to talk about their mistakes and flaws, just like everyone else. They need to talk about their Getting and Protecting Behaviors. They need to see how they sometimes manipulate people by acting like victims. They need to talk about how they use their anger to get people to do what they want. They need to talk about how they run from relationships, because that's an easier way to live than telling the truth about their own mistakes.

People who have been abused need to feel Real Love and then to look outside themselves and love other people, because that's where they'll find true happiness. It's often not an easy process, but the healing is beautiful. Nicole learned to take the steps to find Real Love, and as she felt the acceptance of wise men and women, the pain of her entire life slowly fell away. She learned how to have loving and fulfilling relationships without feeling like a victim.

I know I've said several times that how we respond to other people in the *present* is in large measure determined by how unconditionally loved we feel, and that that is determined by how much Real Love we've received in the *past*. However, we are not slaves to the past. We still have the ability to make our own choices, and *if we can see different choices to make,* we can change the course of our life. If we can find Real Love and share it with others, we can experience great joy despite an unhappy past.

Real Love: The Answer to All Our Relationship "Problems"

Couples often come to me asking for help with their "relationship." What they usually mean is that they want to learn better techniques for manipulating each other, and they've usually tried many other techniques before talking to me. But a relationship really is a natural result of people making independent decisions, and until the partners involved are making loving decisions, no relationship can be loving. Charlotte and Darrell learned that.

After fifteen years of marriage, Charlotte and Darrell were "getting along" fairly well. They had come to believe, as most couples do, that the relative absence of major conflict in their lives meant that they were happy. But they still sensed that something was missing. Charlotte talked to a wise friend about her feelings. "I'm not satisfied with our marriage," she said, "but what can I do about it?"

"Right now?" the wise woman asked. "Probably nothing.

You can't do anything about your *relationship* until you do something about the one person in the relationship you are responsible for: *you*."

Charlotte seemed surprised. "I don't understand. What's wrong with me?"

"I wouldn't choose the word *wrong*," her friend said, "but if you're unhappy, there's always something missing in *your* life, and it's always the same thing. You don't feel loved. From the time you were a child, people liked you better when you did what they wanted. That's natural, but it's *conditional* love. What you really needed—and what you need now—is Real Love, which is *unconditional*. But you didn't get that, and you're not getting it now, and *that's* why you're unhappy. Unconditional love is the only thing in life that can make us genuinely happy."

Her friend continued. "When you got married, you hoped that Darrell would make you happy, which is understandable. But Darrell had never been unconditionally loved, either, so he couldn't give you what you really needed. You both found yourselves in the impossible situation of starving to death and hopelessly demanding to be fed by one another. *That* is why you feel like your relationship is missing something."

They talked until Charlotte understood how her marriage had become the way it was. There was nobody to blame. Charlotte's and Darrell's problems had started long before they even met each other. Once she understood that, Charlotte was able to talk about her Getting and Protecting Behaviors and to recognize how those had caused most of the conflicts that had occurred much more frequently in their marriage than she had originally admitted.

"So it's obvious that Darrell and I need unconditional love," said Charlotte. "Where do we get it?"

"At this point," the wise woman suggested, "it's not likely

that either of you can get the Real Love you need from the other—you've both already demonstrated that you simply don't have it to give. So I suggest that you get it from people who have it. And *you* can only get it for yourself, not for Darrell. As you feel loved, you'll feel that happiness you've been missing all your life, and you'll also feel more loving. You'll have created the possibility of having a more loving *relationship*."

"For you to feel more loved," the wise woman continued, "you have to start consistently telling the truth about yourself to people who can unconditionally accept and love you. You can talk to me, if you'd like, and I'll introduce you to several other people who are capable of listening to you and accepting you. When you feel loved enough, your life will begin to change."

Charlotte wrinkled her forehead and said, "But I thought married people were supposed to love each other, not go to other people for the love they're missing."

"Nothing I'm telling you is meant to detract from your loyalty to your husband," her friend assured her. "In fact, as you feel more Real Love from others, you'll be able to share that with Darrell and it will add a great deal to your marriage. It would be wonderful if all couples could find the love they need *within* their relationship. But sometimes they need help. Unfortunately, not many people have received enough Real Love to be able to share any with their partner. Most partners in relationships simply *can't* give each other the unconditional love they both need, no matter how much they want to.

"Tonight I've learned a lot of things about you," said the wise woman. "You're not as happy as you've always pretended to be. You've admitted that you get angry to protect yourself, and that you do other things to manipulate Darrell. Your marriage is not the success you hoped it would be. And you're not capable of unconditionally loving your husband. But even after sharing all those 'flaws' about yourself, how do you feel now?"

"Relieved—and surprised," Charlotte said. "You've been very gentle and accepting of me. I feel closer to you than ever."

Charlotte's wise friend smiled. "If you'll *keep* telling the truth about yourself with other people who can accept you, that feeling of being loved will grow, and it will change your whole life."

Even though Charlotte felt wonderful during the conversation with her friend, in the following days she forgot the acceptance she'd felt while telling the truth, and she again became afraid to talk openly about herself. That's common for people who are just learning to tell the truth about themselves. It takes more than a little love to eliminate the emptiness and fear of a lifetime.

At first Charlotte chose to handle her relationship with Darrell by herself. But all she had to bring to her well-meaning efforts were the same emptiness and fears she'd always had. She tried to create something new with the same tools, and inevitably her relationship with her husband remained unchanged.

Then, after several months of frustration, Charlotte remembered how good she'd felt being loved by her friend, and she made contact with her again, as well as with other wise men and women. Gradually, she learned to tell the truth about herself on a regular basis and was thrilled at the effect of being seen, accepted, and loved. Even though she was not yet able to love Darrell unconditionally, she was much happier herself. Darrell saw that, and seeing the change in his partner motivated him to start associating with wise men himself. As a result, he, too, found the unconditional acceptance *he'd* always wanted.

As they each continued to tell the truth, Charlotte and Darrell both felt increasingly loved, safe, and happy. The change in their relationship was slow at first, but it was real and lasting. They began to tell the truth to one another; their relationship became more loving, naturally and effortlessly. We *must* get loved ourselves before we can love anyone else, and the process of feeling loved begins with telling the truth about ourselves to people who are capable of accepting and loving us.

It's very important to notice that Charlotte's wise friend was not trying to replace Darrell in Charlotte's life. If you're in a committed relationship, the first person you need to *consider* telling the truth and finding Real Love with is *that* partner. If, for some reason, you feel that's impossible, you can find a wise man somewhere else, but I suggest you do that with the intent of bringing Real Love back to your committed relationship, rather than replacing your partner. Most relationships can change dramatically when one partner is willing to love the other unconditionally. Leaving a committed relationship is rarely the best first step, something we'll talk about much more in Chapters Eight and Nine. I therefore recommend that you choose to talk to wise men for whom you will not feel a sexual attraction. It's very difficult for you to feel Real Love from someone when you're manipulating him or her for sexual attention, and you don't want to do anything that will interfere with your fidelity toward your committed partner. In addition, I suggest that you talk with your partner about your intentions to tell the truth about yourself with others. Your partner may feel jealous or left out, and although you certainly can't control his or her feelings, you can help your partner feel more included by being open and honest about what you're doing. And if he or she continues to resent what you're doing, remember that you're trying to find the Real Love that will fill your life and your relationship with the happiness you've always wanted.

The Need for Consistent Real Love

Like almost everyone, Stacy had been conditionally loved as a child. As a teenager, she'd become increasingly rebellious, and by the time I met her—at age nineteen—she'd been through several miserable relationships with men and was drinking and using drugs.

Stacy called me at the recommendation of a friend. We talked about the mess she'd already made of her life, and she was surprised and delighted at how accepted she felt during our conversation. I recommended that she tell the truth about herself every day, with me and a group of women I thought were capable of loving her. She called me several times in the following weeks, but then she gradually went back to the familiar and reproducible pleasures of Imitation Love, and we lost contact. It's very easy for those first feelings of real acceptance to be overwhelmed by the effects of a lifetime of emptiness and fear.

When Stacy finally called again after a year, she was living with an abusive man and using cocaine every day. We talked in my home. "Life sucks," she said.

"Are you serious about doing something different this time?" I asked.

"What do you mean?"

"Do you remember what I recommended when we talked the last time?"

"Sort of. You said I should talk with some people, but I did that."

"And how often did I suggest that you do that?"

"Are you saying I have to do this your way?" she asked. "That doesn't sound like unconditional love to me."

"I care about your happiness no matter what you do," I assured her. "That's what unconditional love is. But I've also learned that changing a lifetime of unhappiness requires more than a casual effort. If you really want to change the direction of your life, you need to tell the truth about yourself and feel loved *consistently*. When you do that, everything will change. If you do it only occasionally, nothing will happen. But you don't have to do it to please *me*. You don't have to do anything to please me. You'll be doing this for *you*."

Stacy came to my home every day for several weeks after that. And she also called once or twice a day, just for reassurance that she was still loved. One day, she bounced into my office and sat down with a huge grin. She'd broken up with her abusive boyfriend, and she hadn't used any drugs in three weeks. "I'm glad you talked straight to me when I first came to you a few weeks ago," she said. "You didn't exactly say I was being lazy, but I was. I wasn't taking this seriously, and I needed to. Now that I've been talking to you every day, I've been feeling more loved and happy than I ever have in my life." Stacy subsequently learned to develop healthy relationships with many people, and she's now a very happy person.

When we put our whole heart into finding unconditional love, the result is infinitely rewarding. But when we make half an effort, the result is not half of infinite—it's usually nothing at all. Half measures are often worthless, like putting half the wheels on a car.

Real Love is the greatest treasure of all. It's worth whatever effort we expend to find it. It's worth any risk we take. When we tell the truth about ourselves consistently, we create the opportunity for Real Love to completely overpower our emptiness and fear. And then we experience the kind of happiness that becomes our entire reason to live.

> Real Love is the greatest treasure of all. Whatever effort and risk you put into finding it will be well rewarded.

Magnifying the Effect of Real Love with Gratitude

There are few things that contribute more to happiness and loving relationships than gratitude. Without it, we miss all the joy of feeling loved and loving others.

Jack and Patricia had an unsatisfying relationship filled with the exchange of Imitation Love. On the occasions when they got what they wanted from each other, they were relatively "happy." But when their expectations were not met, their disappointment and anger clearly revealed the emptiness of their relationship.

After talking to a wise friend who taught them about Real Love and the process of finding it, Jack started telling the truth about himself and found some loving friends who accepted him unconditionally. As a result, he began to feel genuinely happy for the first time he could remember. Patricia, however, was skeptical and chose to do nothing. After several weeks, they met again with their friend, who asked, "Has either of you noticed any difference in your relationship?"

Patricia said, "No. Jack still watches television all the time and ignores me."

"Jack," the wise man asked, "in the past twenty-four hours, have you spent any time with Patricia?"

"This afternoon, I sat in the kitchen and listened to her talk about what she did all day," Jack said. "I called her from work during my lunch break, just to see how she was doing. And we talked for half an hour in bed last night."

"Patricia, do you remember those things?" asked their friend.

"Well, yes," she said, "but he still sits there in front of the television and . . ."

It's true that Jack still watched a lot of television, but he was learning new things and was beginning to change his feelings and behavior toward Patricia. We don't become loving overnight. We learn to be loving in the same way we learn anything else—we practice, and the progress is gradual. But when we're not grateful for the small steps people take, we don't see their progress, which guarantees that we'll continue to be disappointed and unhappy with them, as Patricia was with Jack.

Being ungrateful is a natural result of having expectations. When we suffer the pain of emptiness and fear, we feel justified in expecting other people to drop what they're doing and help us. But those expectations destroy happiness. When I expect you to give me five apples and you give me only three, I can't possibly be grateful for the three I get. I effectively ruin the enjoyment of your gift by focusing on the two apples I *don't* get. What a pity. When we don't get what we expect, we're always disappointed. And even when we do get what we expect, the best we can feel is "not disappointed," which is the problem with having expectations—it's a lot less fun than feeling loved and being grateful.

Being grateful is a decision we make, and it creates joy in every experience, as Gary and Melissa discovered. They, too, had a relationship filled with Imitation Love, much like Patricia and Jack. Neither intentionally manipulated or hurt the other, but they both used Getting and Protecting Behaviors that made Real Love between them impossible.

They talked to a wise friend, who taught them about Real Love and the process of finding it. Gary started telling the truth about himself to some loving men who accepted him unconditionally. Melissa was too afraid to do the same, but she did choose to believe that Gary was trying to do something different, and she watched him with interest. After several weeks, they met again with their friend, who asked, "Has either of you noticed any change in your relationship?"

"Something is different about Gary," said Melissa. "This afternoon, he sat in the kitchen and listened to me talk about what I did all day. It was great. Earlier, he called from work just to see how I was doing. And we talked for half an hour in bed last night, something we hadn't done in a long time. This is better than Christmas."

"In the past, you complained that he watched television all the time," said their friend. "Does he still do that?"

"Sure," said Melissa, "he still watches TV a lot, but so what? He also spends time with *me,* and it's obvious that he cares about me. I'm loving every minute of this."

Gary turned to Melissa and spoke. "I'm enjoying our time together, too—more than I thought I would. And I love seeing you happier."

Gary didn't do any more for Melissa than Jack did for Patricia, but the results were vastly different for Melissa, because she chose to be grateful for her experiences with Gary instead of complaining about what she didn't get.

Gratitude is not a trick of positive thinking. Gratitude is a *choice* we make to simply acknowledge the truth about what we have, which greatly amplifies our enjoyment of everything we receive.

Patricia's failure to appreciate her husband's efforts was not malicious. She was just empty and afraid to exercise faith that change was possible. But, malicious or not, her choice to be skeptical nonetheless destroyed any possibility of her enjoying a loving experience with Jack. In addition, her ingratitude was discouraging to him, making it harder for him to continue his efforts to love her.

> Gratitude is simply a decision we make to recognize what we already have, and that decision greatly magnifies the effect of the love and happiness in our lives.

In addition to being grateful for the progress we see in others, we need to recognize and be grateful for our own growth. *We* can't become perfectly loving in a day any more than those around us can. We learn with practice, but when we don't recognize the positive steps we take, we tend to become discouraged and stop trying. As you take the steps to find Real Love, you'll change gradually, as Gary, Jack, and Charlotte did. At times, you'll feel peaceful and will be more patient, forgiving, and loving toward the people around you. But at other times, you'll go back to your old Getting and Protecting Behaviors. Be grateful for your own progress, rather than discouraged by your mistakes. If you can be grateful for your successes without being proud in an egotistical sense, your gratitude will magnify your happiness and build your faith.

Sadly, most of us learned a form of gratitude that can actually interfere with happiness. From childhood, we were taught to be grateful *to* the people who did things for us. If we failed to express our gratitude when people gave us an ice cream cone or birthday gift, for example, some adult usually admonished, "Now, what do you say?" In effect, we were forced to say thank-you to the people who gave us anything.

Regrettably, that approach usually taught us unfortunate lessons, both as the receiver of those "gifts" and later when we gave them. When we were pressured to be grateful, we didn't experience feelings of love and happiness; what we felt was a sense of *obligation*. It's difficult to feel unconditionally loved by people who *require* an expression of gratitude when they give us something. Of course, we then learned to demand the same gratitude from others, for the same reason it was required of us—it temporarily feels good to have people be grateful *to* us. When people give us their gratitude, we feel gracious and generous. And so we often use the gratitude of others as a form of Imitation Love.

In contrast, it's quite healthy to be grateful *for* what we have. That kind of gratitude magnifies the enjoyment of every experience and opportunity. With it, we feel energized, hopeful, and happy. When we're grateful, envy and disappointment disappear, and we feel closer to the people who love us as well as to those we love.

Sharing Your Fortune

The Power of Loving Others

The joy of being loved is indescribable, but the joy of unconditionally loving others is even greater. Fortunately,
learning to love others becomes a simple process once we feel
unconditionally loved ourselves. When we feel loved, we're
no longer blinded by emptiness and fear, and then we can *see*
other people clearly. When we see people as they really are,
accepting them becomes natural and effortless. As we accept
people—without criticism or expectation—we unavoidably
develop a concern for their happiness, and that is the definition of *Real Love*.

As with becoming loved, learning to love others is a four-
step process, which can be summarized as follows: Loved →
Seeing → Accepting → Loving.

Loved: We Can't Give What We Don't Have

We must understand the importance of finding and *feeling*
Real Love before we can *give* it. We can't give what we don't

have, and if we don't understand that, there will be many occasions when we'll attempt to love someone only to discover that we've just made the situation worse with our Getting and Protecting Behaviors. Michelle learned about the need to feel loved in the following way.

She and her husband constantly manipulated each other for approval and defended themselves against each other's criticism. When Michelle attended a seminar I taught on the subject of relationships, she dutifully wrote down what I said and eagerly went home to try out what she'd learned. She called me a few days later. "At your workshop," she said, "you gave examples of what some couples have said to each other as they were learning to be truthful and loving. I tried to say some of those things to my husband, but they didn't work at all. He actually got angry at me. It was awful."

"What did you say to him?" I asked.

"Well, I tried several things," Michelle said, "but I'll tell you about one of them. Yesterday after we both came home from work, he started complaining about things. That usually ends up in an argument. He started off complaining about something his boss had said to him, and then he started in on the kids' last report cards—like that was all *my* fault. I'm tired of him taking his frustration out on me. So instead of getting into an argument—which is what we usually do—I tried to *see him* and *love him* like you suggested. I said, 'You seem angry.' I was trying to give him a chance to tell the truth about himself and feel accepted, but he didn't take it that way at all. He just blew up even worse."

"Think for a moment," I suggested, "about what it meant when you said to me just now, 'I'm tired of him taking his frustration out on me.' Is that a concern for *his* happiness— which is Real Love—or is it a concern for *yourself*?"

"But I *am* concerned about him," she said.

"Yes, *part* of you is—I believe that. But a big part of you is *angry* at him, and you were angry at him *then*, too. He *felt* that, and when he sensed your anger, he felt even more unloved, and then he reacted by protecting himself with more anger of his own."

"But I wasn't angry," insisted Michelle.

"Sure you were," I replied gently. "You said you were *tired* of him taking his frustration out on you. That's just another way of saying that you were *angry*."

"But I didn't *show* it," she said. "I spoke to him very nicely."

I chuckled. "Remember that I'm not criticizing you. I'm trying to get you to see something that will help you more than you can imagine. This insight can change your whole life. Although you don't think you showed your anger, it was steaming out of your ears, flashing from your eyes, and communicating very clearly from your posture and tone of voice. We think we hide our anger, but we really don't. When you first got on the phone with me, you were irritated with your husband. Your tone of voice was filled with anger. And if *I* felt it, I *promise* you that your husband felt it."

Michelle didn't respond, so I continued. "Actually, you were a little irritated with *me*, too, because the things I had talked about in the seminar had failed to help your marriage. Take a deep breath and understand that when you get angry at me, it really doesn't annoy or hurt me. However, your anger *is* hurting you and your marriage, and I'd like to help you to see what you're doing and change it."

There was a long silence as Michelle made a decision about whether she would feel accepted or criticized by me. She finally sighed and said, "Okay, so what do I do now?" This was a big moment. Michelle had decided I wasn't attacking her.

"I know you were trying to love your husband," I assured

her. "But do you remember the first step in learning to love other people?"

"No," she replied.

"You have to feel loved yourself," I said, "before you can love your husband and hope to change your relationship."

"But I do feel loved," she objected.

"I know you believe that, but it's simply not possible. If you had felt unconditionally loved, you would not have felt disappointed and angry when your husband didn't respond the way you wanted. You felt disappointed because you were already empty, and your anger was a reaction to that emptiness. If you had really felt loved, the way he reacted wouldn't have bothered you at all." We then talked about what she could do to find Real Love for herself.

> We can't love other people unconditionally until we've felt unconditionally loved ourselves. We can't give what we don't have.

When I say we must feel loved before we can give love, I intend that only as an *explanation* for our inability to love people in difficult situations—like the one Michelle experienced. I do not mean to provide us an *excuse* for not loving people. If that were true, we could spend a lifetime selfishly sitting on our backsides, looking for and taking in the love of other people, saying, "But I'm not ready to love anyone else. I need to feel more love myself first." Later in this chapter, we'll talk more about loving people even when we feel incapable of doing so.

We also need to understand that loving other people usually does not involve telling them the truth about *themselves,* as Michelle was trying to do. Loving others is usually demonstrated by unspoken acceptance or quiet acts of kindness. Occasionally, partners in mutually loving relationships may tell the truth about one another, but that requires more love and experience than Michelle had yet acquired so early in her quest to find and give Real Love, and it's something we'll be discussing further in the following chapter.

Seeing: The Elimination of Our Own Blindness

We see people clearly when we see them as they really are—with their needs, fears, flaws, and strengths—instead of seeing what we want from them or fear from them. And we must see people clearly before we can love them unconditionally.

When we don't feel loved ourselves—when we're empty and afraid—we can't see people clearly; we can see only what they might do *to* us or *for* us. Our vision is impaired, and that condition inevitably leads to expectations, disappointment, and intolerance.

While we're experiencing the unbearable pain of feeling unloved, we're blind to other people's needs and feel justified in expecting them to give us whatever we think *we* need to alleviate our discomfort. As a result, we simply cannot tolerate anyone who will not help us. But most of the people around us don't feel unconditionally loved, either, so they're naturally focused entirely on filling *their own* needs. In that condition, they're incapable of giving us the happiness we expect, and they'll even do things that inconvenience and hurt us. Our disappointment in others—and conflict with them—is therefore guaranteed.

Another effect of being unable to see people clearly is that they effectively disappear. When we see them only as objects that either serve or hurt us, who they really are does not exist for us. Obviously, we are then alone, the very condition we fear the most.

―――――

We can learn to see people clearly. But it's not a technique we learn from a book. Our failure to see is a natural result of the blinding effects of emptiness and fear. *Seeing clearly is, therefore, the natural result of eliminating emptiness and fear with Real Love.* No other approach to seeing and loving will work until we address our need for Real Love.

As we begin to feel unconditionally loved, however, there are some additional resources we can use to help us see even better and more quickly. When we remember the Rules of Seeing described in Chapter Four, our ability to see people clearly is enhanced considerably. I especially encourage you to recall the Fourth Rule: "If you can't be a wise man, get one." When we're unhappy in a relationship, we're invariably having difficulty seeing our partner clearly. A wise friend can help us to see that partner more clearly and so to move along on the path toward accepting and loving him or her.

When we see people without distortion, we cease to feel threatened and alone. We realize that all the "unattractive" behaviors of human beings—attacking, accusing, manipulating, selfishness, anger, and so on—are just reactions to their own emptiness and fear. When we feel loved, we no longer find people "ugly" when they use their Getting and Protecting Behaviors—we see that they're just drowning and trying to survive.

When I first knew Richard, he was always angry about something, and people tended to avoid him. Because I met him at a time when I, too, felt unloved and unhappy, I also judged him harshly and avoided him. As I learned to tell the truth about myself, however, I felt more loved and was less blinded by my own emptiness and fear, and I came to realize that Richard was not intentionally being offensive; he was just afraid and attacking people to protect himself. He became a different person entirely when I saw him clearly.

The world is a much more beautiful place when we see it clearly, as are the people who live in it. That clarity of vision changes our relationships dramatically. For example, when you see your partner clearly, and he or she becomes critical or angry, you know he or she is only afraid and protecting himself or herself. With that understanding, it no longer makes sense to be resentful or angry, and without resentment and anger, relationships naturally become more loving.

We can also turn this same clear-sightedness inward, upon ourselves. Our own anger and selfishness are also reactions to emptiness and fear, which means it would be just as foolish to feel excessively guilty or ashamed about our own mistakes as it is to be angry at others for getting Imitation Love and protecting themselves. Without Real Love, we're all doing the only things we know to survive.

Some guilt is useful. It motivates us to move away from behaviors that are harmful to ourselves and others. But we don't need to feel excessively guilty for the mistakes we unavoidably make as we learn to be loving, even when those mistakes cause pain for our children, spouses, and others. That unnecessary burden of guilt causes *us* a pain that ensures we will use Getting and Protecting Behaviors instead of telling the truth about ourselves, and then we become incapable of feeling loved and loving others.

How we see the world entirely determines what we say and do. As we feel unconditionally loved and learn to see clearly, the whole world changes before our eyes, and loving other people becomes a natural and effortless consequence. When that happens, we feel an immediate connection to everyone with whom we interact, and then we are no longer alone.

Accepting: The Natural, Peaceful Result of Seeing

There are only two reasons we don't accept people as they are:

1. We *want* something from them and don't get it. When we feel unloved, we cannot accept anyone who fails to give us what we want.
2. We're *afraid* of them because they're criticizing, mocking, or avoiding us—or because they *might* do those things. How can we possibly accept someone we're afraid of?

In short, we don't accept people because *we* are empty and afraid. The solution to our intolerance is obvious. We need to feel unconditionally loved, which will eliminate our emptiness and fear, and then it will be easy for us to see people as they are—instead of as objects to be used or feared—and accept them.

Ellis was critical of just about everyone: black people, poor people, his neighbors, women, fat people, foreigners, politicians, policemen, and so on. But he had one friend who could see that he was just unloved, empty, and afraid, and this wise friend taught Ellis about Real Love and the effects it could have on his life. Ellis found some of what his friend had to say difficult to believe.

"Are you saying," asked Ellis, "that if I felt loved and saw people clearly, I'd love everybody?"

"Yes," answered his friend.

Ellis burst out laughing. "No way. I could never love a woman who was ugly and fat."

The wise man smiled as he spoke. "Without feeling unconditionally loved yourself, you see other people only as a potential source of Imitation Love—praise, power, pleasure, and safety. You see them as a way of filling your emptiness.

I'm your friend, and I tell you this because I care about you. When you look at a woman, you're too selfish to see who she really is. You see only how she might make *you* happy—by giving you something beautiful to look at, by flattering you, or by becoming an object for your sexual fantasies. If a woman offers you those things, you like her. That's Imitation Love, because your concern is for *your* happiness, not hers. You don't love 'ugly, fat' women because they can't give you the kind of Imitation Love you want."

Ellis frowned, so his friend assured him, "I'm not criticizing you in any way. I'm just describing what you're doing. When you get enough Real Love, you won't be empty all the time, and therefore you won't see people only as objects that either are or are not capable of filling your emptiness. You'll be able to see who people really are, and then you'll see that everyone really is beautiful. You'll accept people instead of rejecting them because of their supposedly 'unattractive' physical features."

Without Real Love, we see people only as objects that will or will not give us what we want. When they don't, we reject them and criticize them for being too rich, poor, tall, short, black, white, fat, skinny, beautiful, unattractive, and so on. It's the lack of love in *our own* lives that causes all the disgust, prejudice, racism, and hatred in the world.

> It's the lack of Real Love in our individual lives that causes all the anger, racism, and contention in the world.

Most of us *say* we accept our partners, but our behavior says otherwise.

Rick and Mary had been married for several years and had become increasingly dissatisfied with their relationship. After trying unsuccessfully to improve matters on their own, they finally decided to discuss their situation with a wise friend. Once they were all seated in his living room, Mary began speaking. "I'm not happy with our relationship."

"In what way would you like it to be different?" asked the wise man.

"I wish Rick could just accept me and not criticize everything I do," answered Mary.

"But I do accept you," said Rick.

"No, you don't," countered Mary. "You're always telling me what's wrong with me—you think I'm overweight, I spend too much time at work, I spend too much money on things you don't agree with, and whenever we talk about the kids, you—"

The wise man knew it probably wouldn't help either of them to hear the entire list of Rick's critical comments, so he interrupted and asked, "Rick, do you say those things?"

"Hardly ever," Rick answered.

The wise man turned to Mary for clarification. "Mary?"

"He doesn't usually say it with words," said Mary, "but it's all over his face and in his tone of voice whenever those subjects come up. And when he's angry, he stays in another room and doesn't touch me."

"Rick, are you aware that you do those things?" asked the wise man.

"Not really," said Rick.

"I believe that," said the wise man. "We've been friends for years, so I know you've felt unloved and empty all your life. Feeling like that, it's understandable that you'd become disappointed whenever Mary didn't do exactly what you wanted— like when she stays at work for long hours or spends money in ways you don't understand. Without being aware of it, you communicate that disappointment to her in many ways, and she feels it. I know what I'm talking about; I used to do that to my wife all the time."

The wise man went on to explain why expectations and disappointment were poisoning their relationship. He also made it clear that Rick's disappointment was not Mary's fault—he was reacting to a lifetime of not feeling loved.

We generally don't accept people as they are. We say we do. We wish we did. We know we should. But we don't, and we prove that with our behavior.

———

Disappointment is one of the most common ways we demonstrate our lack of acceptance toward our partners. Without Real Love, we're miserable, and then we naturally expect our partners to help us feel better by giving us what we want. When they don't, we're disappointed. We tend to believe that other people exist for the primary purpose of making us happy, and when they don't, we judge their behavior to be unacceptable.

Disappointment is so common among people that we believe it's a normal and unavoidable reaction to not getting what we want. We're disappointed if other drivers aren't courteous, if our boss isn't appreciative, if our spouse isn't cooperative and loving, if our children aren't sufficiently grateful, and so on. What we need to understand is that disappointment is absolute proof that we don't accept people and things the way they are, and it's always selfish and wrong.

Rachel and Vicki had been friends for years, but Vicki was becoming increasingly irritated with Rachel, and she talked about her irritation with a wise friend. "Whenever we talk on the phone," Vicki said, "it's only because *I* make the call. Rachel never calls *me*."

This wise woman understood that when we're unhappy, *we* are not feeling loved and are therefore incapable of loving our partner. Vicki's friend smiled as she said, "The problem here is that you don't accept Rachel as she is."

Vicki was not expecting that answer. "But I do accept her. I just don't like the fact that she never calls me."

"How do you feel when Rachel doesn't call you?" asked the wise woman.

"I'm disappointed and hurt. How could I not be?"

"When you're disappointed," said the wise woman, "Rachel correctly hears that she has failed to meet your expectations and is therefore not acceptable to you. She hears that you want her to change who she is to make *you* happy. Your concern is for *your* happiness, not hers—and she feels that."

Because Vicki trusted that her wise friend cared about her, she listened and realized that she did want Rachel to change. As she told the truth about her selfishness, she felt accepted by this wise woman. Feeling loved *with* her flaws gave Vicki a sense of peace and happiness that enabled her to see and accept Rachel.

———

For many years, my own sighs and frowns of disappointment communicated this message to my children: "I accept you only when you do what I want. When you don't, I love you less." That's what disappointment means. Most of us heard that message from our parents, and we've passed it on to our spouses, children, friends, co-workers, and others. We don't intend to do it, but we nonetheless declare with our disappointment that our partners are defective and unacceptable.

When children sense that we don't accept them, they believe something is wrong with them. As adults, most of us carry scars from many interactions during which our parents and others told us we had disappointed them. That's why we learned to protect ourselves with lies, anger, acting like victims, and running. That's why we learned to seek the pleasures of Imitation Love with Getting and Protecting Behaviors.

People look for excuses to justify their disappointment, but that can be dangerous. A woman once said to me, "I don't think all disappointment is selfish and wrong. For example, what if I worked all day to prepare a picnic to take to the park, and then it rained, spoiling my plans. I don't think it would be selfish to be disappointed in a situation like that." We *could* make a distinction between disappointment with *things* or circumstances and disappointment with people, justifying the former and condemning the latter. But I've seen the results of that ethical hair-splitting. It's too easy to go from being disappointed in some thing or circumstance to being disappointed in someone else's behavior, and then to fool ourselves into believing that we can separate the way we feel about the person from the way we feel about his or her actions. In fact, when we say, "I'm only disappointed in my partner's *behavior,* not in my *partner,*" that distinction is actually a self-deceptive justification, because *any* form of disappointment will continue to prevent us from being happy in our relationships.

When I say that disappointment is always selfish and wrong, I'm not saying that we're evil or worthy of punishment when we're disappointed. I understand that if you don't feel sufficiently loved, disappointment is entirely natural. But remember, I've also said that anything that interferes with our ability to feel loved, loving, or happy is wrong, and disappointment always does that. Granted, it is *understandable* that you'd become disappointed if it rained and spoiled your picnic, but as you experience more Real Love, you'll find that your disappointment will be displaced by feelings of gratitude for the love you already have. The more unconditionally loved we feel, the less disappointed we'll be in the outcome of any particular circumstance or activity.

Anger is a tiny step beyond disappointment, and is always selfish and unloving. As long as we feel angry, we can't have a loving relationship with anyone.

> Disappointment and anger are selfish. You can't be genuinely loving toward your partner if you're disappointed or angry with him or her.

When we attempt to control our partner's behavior, we demonstrate in yet another way that we don't accept him or her. We deny his right to make his own choices and learn in his own way. That violates the Law of Choice, which we've discussed earlier, and is not unconditional acceptance, without which we can't possibly have a loving relationship. If, on the other hand, we understand and remember that we all have a sacred, inviolable right to choose for ourselves what we think, say, and do—and to make our own mistakes—we'll be able to accept other people more easily, even if they inconvenience or hurt us.

When we "fall in love," the flow of Imitation Love can be generous and satisfying, and we might easily believe we're accepting our partner when the truth is that we're just getting what we want from him or her. But the conditional nature of our acceptance becomes obvious on those occasions when we don't get what we want. It's easy to confuse satisfaction with genuine acceptance.

One of the most obvious, and most common, signs of acceptance in a relationship is the absence of criticism. We've already observed how unhappy Mary became when Rick reacted negatively to her appearance, her spending, and her long work hours. She was miserable in spite of the fact that

Rick gave her expensive presents on her birthday, their anniversary, Christmas, Valentine's Day, and sometimes for no special reason. She and Rick also went on vacations together. Although Rick tried to do loving things for Mary in many different ways, all his efforts were forgotten when he criticized her. On those occasions, Mary was devastated. She knew his criticism meant that he wanted her to be a different person, and she was right—that's the only thing criticism delivered with irritation *can* mean.

Rick had never felt unconditionally loved himself, and in his emptiness he naturally demanded that Mary do things to make him happy. When she failed—to be home so he could have someone to talk to, to share the discipline of the children, or to be more physically attractive to him—he became disappointed and made comments intended to prevent her from disappointing him further, as well as to get her to give him what he wanted. In the absence of Real Love, he wanted her to make him happy with Imitation Love, and his reaction to her failure was understandable. But he didn't realize how much he was hurting her and their relationship, and he didn't know how to be more loving. Nor did she. Neither of them could see that they were locked in a mutually destructive struggle to find happiness in impossible ways.

Then Rick learned to tell the truth about himself and found people who accepted and loved him. Real Love slowly filled the gaping emptiness that had always motivated him to focus on his own needs. During the times when he felt unconditionally loved, he felt full, complete, and happy, and because he then had what was most important in life, he lost the *need* to make other people give him what he thought he wanted from moment to moment. He discovered that Mary didn't have to be home by a certain time in order for him to be happy. She didn't have to lose weight or do every other little thing he wanted in order to make his world acceptable. He learned that Mary was beautiful just as she was, and as he began to care about her happiness, she could feel it.

One evening Mary got home an hour later than she'd indicated she would, which caused the family an inconvenience because it was her night to provide dinner, a responsibility that she and Rick shared. She finally raced through the door with apologies and a bag of Chinese food, which everyone quickly devoured. After dinner, Mary touched Rick on the arm and said, "You haven't said anything about me coming home late for quite a while. And I know Chinese isn't your favorite takeout, but it was the best I could do at the last minute. You didn't say anything about that, either."

Rick smiled, hung his head, then looked her in the eye. "Sometimes I can't believe the things I've said to you. I just needed someone to make me happy, so I snapped at you whenever you did anything I didn't like. It's embarrassing to me now, and I'm sorry."

Tears poured down Mary's face as she could feel that Rick—at least in that moment—didn't need her to change in order to make him happy. He honestly accepted her as she was. That was the first of many such intimate moments.

When we genuinely accept other people, our behavior changes in any number of ways. For example, when people make mistakes that inconvenience us, we almost always expect them to apologize, and then we generously consider whether or not we'll bless them with our forgiveness. But if you truly accept someone, why would you ever require him to apologize to you for making the mistakes that are unavoidable in the process of learning? You learned from making mistakes, and so will your partner. People really do have the right to make their own choices, including the ones that inconvenience *you*. Demanding an apology is therefore selfish and arrogant, and in any case it will make *you* unhappy.

Gene seemed to be angry much of the time. He was always fussing at someone about a mistake he or she had made, or making critical comments behind someone's back. One day I noticed him scowling and said, "You seem irritated."

"Of course," he replied, and went on to describe how thoughtless and stupid his boss had been that day.

"Who else at work is causing problems?" I asked. Without hesitation, he began to rattle off a long list of names. With tongue in cheek, I asked, "What kind of job is your wife doing at home, as a wife and mother?"

He didn't understand that I was teasing him, of course, so he responded with a detailed accounting of her many mistakes and flaws.

"It sounds to me," I said, "like almost everyone you know owes you a huge apology."

Gene looked surprised. "What do you mean?"

"We all make mistakes. It's the human condition. It's unavoidable. So do you. When you get angry, whether you realize it or not, you're saying that people—in this case a lot of people—have dared to commit the crime of inconveniencing Your Royal Highness. And you expect some kind of apology from them. You want them to stop being who they are—with all their inconvenient flaws—and make things right with *you*."

Gene could easily have taken what I said as an attack, but we'd been friends for some time, so instead he mulled it over in his mind for a moment. Finally, he said, "I never thought about it like that. I guess I can be pretty demanding."

When we truly accept our partners, we understand that they must make mistakes in the process of learning. They will, and so will we. When we accept them, we don't insist that they apologize. We have faith that as they see their mistakes more clearly, they'll be less likely to repeat them. Our relationships will become much happier when we decide not to require apologies from our partners, but instead to apologize ourselves (which really means to tell the truth about our mistakes) and to quickly forgive (which really means to accept) our partners. By learning to give your partner the gift of your acceptance you'll bring great joy into your own life, and you'll experience an enormous change in your relationship.

While you're looking for the Real Love that will allow you to become naturally accepting, you can also exercise some simple self-control. When your partner leaves the cap off the toothpaste, for example, think about it before you open your mouth. Do you want to save a few cents on toothpaste, or do you want to start having a profoundly loving and rewarding relationship? Is there really a question in your mind about that? Do you really want the short-term satisfaction you might get from criticizing your partner and possibly changing any specific, superficially annoying behavior, even though you now know that your criticism might damage your potentially loving and mutually rewarding, long-term relationship? Think about it before you open your mouth about anything.

When we accept our partners, *they* will feel loved and happier—and so will we. Trying to change other people is a lot of work. Expectations, disappointment, blaming, and anger are exhausting. When we eliminate those behaviors and accept people as they are, what remains is a deeply satisfying peace. And real acceptance is effortless; it flows naturally once we feel loved.

But does acceptance mean we can never ask for what we want? Does it mean we have to lie down like a doormat and put up with everything our partner does? No, not at all. We can still make *requests* for what we want, say *no* when people make their own requests or demands, and insist that people not do harmful things *to* us. We'll talk more about those situations in Chapters Seven and Nine.

Acceptance also doesn't mean approval of bad behavior. It's possible to identify and condemn unloving and destructive behavior while still accepting the person exhibiting that behavior. But that's *not* what most people do, despite their vigorous claims to the contrary. It's quite common for people—especially parents—to say, "I love you, but I'm angry at your behavior." *That is a lie* we use to justify our anger. When we genuinely accept someone, we never feel disappointment or anger as we describe their mistakes. When people feel unconditionally loved, *they don't get angry.*

Imposing Consequences

One evening I realized that my favorite pen was missing. When I asked my children if anyone had seen it, Benjamin said, "I borrowed it. I took it to school, and now I can't find it."

Years before, I would have been furious. When I felt empty, any inconvenience was enough to increase my pain to the point where I lashed out to stop the inconvenience and punish the poor soul who had dared to cause it. On this occasion, however, I had the benefit of years of feeling loved. I was full and happy—I had a metaphorical twenty million dollars in the bank—and in that condition this small inconvenience meant nothing.

My son, however, still needed to learn from his mistake, so I continued. "Tell me what your mistake was."

Benjamin had participated in many family discussions about telling the truth and being responsible, so he realized that when he had admitted borrowing the pen and losing it, he hadn't told the whole truth. "I was selfish," he said. "I needed a pen, so I took one from your desk without thinking about you at all. When I lost it, I didn't want to get in trouble, so I didn't tell you about it. I hid my mistake, and that's lying."

"Excellent," I said. "You know what you did wrong, and now you're less likely to make those choices again. I'm happy for you. How do you feel now?"

"Relieved. I always feel better when I tell the truth and you still love me."

Benjamin lost my pen because he made a selfish choice, and he needed to see that. But if I'd been angry at him, I would *not* have been loving *him* and condemning *his behavior*. I have corrected my children in anger on many occasions, and it is always wrong. I've tried to justify my behavior by saying that I was angry only at their behavior, not at them, and it was always a lie. My being angry at Benjamin would not have helped him in any way; it would only have hurt him and our relationship. What he needed to know was that he'd made a mistake—which on this occasion he knew without my telling him—and that I accepted and loved him *while* he was being irresponsible and inconvenient. If he hadn't understood his mistake, it would have been my responsibility to point it out, but without disappointment and anger. He had learned an important lesson the same way I've learned most of my lessons—by making mistakes. I accepted that—and him. People learn far better while feeling loved than they do while feeling our anger.

Anger is never justifiable. It always demonstrates a lack of acceptance. But accepting people doesn't mean that we can't impose consequences for their poor choices. For example, if a child carelessly wrecks the family car—which has happened in our family—he might benefit from paying the increase in insurance premiums that results from the accident, or he might not be allowed to drive for a specified time.

In an ideal society—if everyone were unconditionally loving—imposing consequences would be entirely unnecessary. When people made mistakes, they would see them, admit them, and try not to make them again. But we don't live in such a place. Instead of learning from their mistakes, many people lie about them and insist on repeating them, even when they injure those around them. And that's why consequences must sometimes be imposed—to *require* people to experience some negative effect from their behavior in the hope that it will motivate them not to repeat that behavior. Sometimes the offender can't be motivated and must simply be restrained so that the rights of others are protected. That's one purpose of prisons.

However, we must be careful how we impose consequences. If we apply them with anger, they become punishments, which rarely benefit anyone. Punishment only heightens the fear and anger of the person being punished, which makes him even more likely to use Getting and Protecting Behaviors in the future. He is then *more* likely—not less—to require future punishment, and when that happens, we haven't helped anyone.

When we punish others in anger, we also hurt ourselves, because anything that interferes with our ability to feel loved and to love others is bad. Although it's true that even the most loving consequences will not change the behavior of some angry people, we who administer them still benefit greatly as we apply them in a loving way. Being loving is always happier than every other way of being.

I would also suggest that you consider imposing consequences on someone only when you are certain that you have a *responsibility* to modify that person's behavior—when you're that person's parent, employer, or parole officer, to name just a few examples. If you attempt to impose consequences on someone whom you don't have direct responsibility for teaching or leading—such as a spouse or a friend—the risk is that you're likely to introduce unnecessary conflict into your relationship.

I should point out, however, that no matter how wisely we impose consequences, they will not always have a positive effect. Some people will still *receive* them as punishments, in much the same way that some people turn Real Love into Imitation Love by receiving it with Getting and Protecting Behaviors. If you lovingly impose a consequence on me, but I decide to see you as an enemy and resist you, I will *feel* your consequence as a punishment.

Accepting someone does not mean we're obliged to spend time with him. For example, when I feel loved, I can easily accept someone who uses dangerous drugs and is violent. I know that he is simply choosing Getting and Protecting Behaviors because he feels unloved and afraid. But I have no obligation to spend my free time with him. As I've said more than once, we all get to make our own choices, and if someone chooses not to give up Getting and Protecting Behaviors that we consider dangerous or simply distasteful, it's always our right—and sometimes our best choice—to walk away from that relationship. We'll talk more about leaving relationships in Chapter Nine.

Loving: Caring About the Happiness of Other People

The entire purpose of relationships is to provide opportunities for us to practice loving each other and to experience the profound joy that always follows.

After one of my seminars, I was approached by Marilyn, a woman who had spoken to me on previous occasions about finding Real Love. "Are you saying," she asked, "that after we feel sufficiently loved ourselves, we'll be able to love *everyone* we know?"

"Yes," I replied. "Of course, that takes time, but as you become filled with Real Love yourself, and as you consciously practice loving others, eventually you will be able to unconditionally love all the people around you."

"That seems a little overwhelming to me," she said.

As we talked for a few moments, I understood the source of her confusion. She thought that when she felt loved, she should then feel obligated to perform acts of service for everyone she knew. She pictured herself becoming the Gandhi or Mother Teresa of her community, and understandably she wasn't sure she wanted that responsibility.

"What is the definition of Real Love?" I asked her.

"Caring about the happiness of another person," she said.

"Right, and you can do that in many ways," I suggested. "Acts of service are just one way. You can also love people by forgiving them for their past offenses, or by quietly accepting them with their differences and flaws. You can love someone by simply having a genuine concern for his or her happiness. You may never even meet some of the people for whom you feel unconditional love. I've often experienced powerful feelings of love toward people for whom I have not actually *done* anything. So can you."

Marilyn had asked a variation on the question "What's the difference between accepting and loving?" Acceptance means forgiving and the absence of criticism, anger, and controlling, while unconditional loving is a more active, outwardly directed caring about the happiness of others that also *includes* acceptance. I can illustrate the difference between accepting and loving by continuing from Chapter Three the story of Joan and Tyler, who, as you may remember, were having quite a conflict over Tyler's unwillingness to pick up after himself at home. I promised you at the end of Chapter Three that I'd later be discussing what Joan might have done if Tyler never chose to change his ways, and I haven't forgotten that promise.

Joan carefully considered the three choices described by her wise friend: to live with it and like it, live with it and hate it, or leave the relationship. She decided that she didn't want to give up her entire relationship with Tyler over some socks and underwear on the floor, and she realized it would be foolish to choose to live in a relationship where she was angry and unhappy all the time. So she chose to have faith in what her friend had said about the existence of Real Love, and she began to tell the truth about herself to people who were capable of loving her.

Gradually, Joan began to experience the fullness and peace that come from receiving Real Love. She had taken the first step in the process of learning to love others (Loved → Seeing → Accepting → Loving). Tyler did continue to leave his clothes and other things around the house, but Joan just didn't care as much as she used to. Joan stopped being angry at Tyler and *accepted* him as he was. She put his things away without saying a word and discovered that the effort required was really quite minimal. Eventually, as her anger faded, she found that she actually *cared more about his happiness*—a significant step beyond simply accepting him with his flaws. She not only stopped nagging him about his messiness, but she also began to do more things for him. She realized she had been avoiding him physically and started touching him more often.

Tyler certainly felt the change in the kind of affection he was getting from Joan, and that had an effect on *his* behavior. Although he hadn't done it *consciously*, one reason Tyler had continued to leave his clothes around the house was to punish Joan. Sure, he was also plain lazy, but part of his motivation for not picking up his things was to "pay her back" for all the nagging and criticizing he received. As he felt more loved, he lost his need to punish her, and he began to pick up his things more often than he had before.

Now, please picture in your mind a partner who is sometimes inconsiderate, thoughtless, or unkind. Sometimes you just don't like being around that person. But as you gain more experience with Real Love, you'll get to the point where you don't need *that one person* to behave in any particular way in order for you to be happy. When you don't need him or her to do anything *for* you or stop doing anything *to* you, you can begin to understand that his behavior is not intended to irritate you personally. You can begin to *see* who he really is. Now that you don't desperately need that person, you can begin to accept him as he is, without criticizing him, manipulating him, or being angry at him. But that may not happen immediately. It takes time for many of us to lose our critical and angry feelings, even after we begin to see other people more clearly.

Now the last step, the big one. When we genuinely accept people unconditionally, it *is* natural for us to begin to care about their happiness—but again, that often takes time. There's a big difference between simply being "not angry" at your partner (a form of acceptance) and really caring that he or she is happy (Real Love).

As I said to Marilyn, Real Love can be demonstrated in many ways. You can give Real Love while sitting in your chair and feeling a genuine concern for the well-being of someone you can't see. But you can also do more tangible things to tell people that you care about their happiness. You know what your partner enjoys—a touch, a loving glance, a small gift, a gentle word, time alone, an apology, an act of service. As you do those things for him or her, you will create opportunities for your partner to feel unconditionally loved, and you will be happier, too.

You need to keep in mind, however, that it won't be ultimately productive to love and accept your partner *so that* he'll do something for you. Joan didn't accept and love Tyler as a *means* of getting him to pick up his things around the house. That was just a fortunate side effect of her love for him. When you love *unconditionally*, you don't expect anything in return.

> Acceptance is forgiving and the absence of criticism, anger, and controlling. Unconditional love is a more active, outwardly directed caring about the happiness of others that also *includes* acceptance.

We *learn* to love just like we learn anything else. It takes time and practice, and in the beginning we won't do it very well. We'll stumble many times, especially on the first step in the process—feeling loved ourselves. And, as we've already discussed, we don't need to feel excessively guilty about that. When we feel unconditionally loved, it's natural and easy for us to accept and love the people around us. But when we're first experiencing Real Love, those few moments of acceptance are opposed by a lifetime of *not* feeling loved. Sometimes—because love is a powerful force—those loving moments are sufficient to overcome the effects of our past, and then we do feel loved and capable of loving others. But when the environment becomes too stressful—when we're with people who are too demanding and critical—we often forget about those who love us. We just *forget*. And then, without thinking, we become afraid and go back to the old and familiar Getting and Protecting Behaviors. In that condition, we're unable to love anyone.

But as we continue to tell the truth about ourselves and feel more loved, our confidence grows and we forget less easily, so that we become capable of loving other people better and more consistently. However, we also need to make *conscious decisions to remember* the unconditional love we've received. Simply by doing that, we will often be less affected by the unloving behavior of those around us. Sandra is a woman who discovered, while interacting with her husband, the inevitability of making mistakes in the process of learning to love others.

Sandra had been learning how to tell the truth about herself for several months. She'd experienced some wonderful moments of unconditional love, and she was beginning to see and accept her husband, Charles.

One afternoon Charles came home in a bad mood and was unpleasant to Sandra. In the past, she would have been angry about that, or she would have avoided him entirely. But because she was feeling loved, Sandra remained happy and didn't feel threatened by Charles's behavior. She then tried to help him feel better, but he resisted everything she did and actually became more irritated. Eventually, it was more than Sandra could handle. She said something hateful and stomped out of the room. She called a wise friend on the phone and told her what had happened. "I don't think I'll ever get this," Sandra said. "Just when I thought I'd learned something about being loving, I blew up again. I'm disgusted with myself and discouraged."

"I've made many mistakes like that," said the wise woman, "and I'll make many more. So will you. You don't need to feel guilty about it. Just see the truth of what you did and know that you're loved while you're making mistakes."

"I guess I'm feeling too stupid to feel loved," Sandra objected.

"As you started talking to Charles this evening, you did feel loved," the wise woman reminded her, "and because of that you were able to reach out to him and try to help him. You cared about his happiness, and that's Real Love. But you've only recently begun to feel loved yourself, so when Charles kept being angry, you felt threatened and briefly forgot that you were loved. It was simply too much for you at this stage in your growth, so you went back to protecting yourself with anger. That's natural. Now you're feeling guilty about mistakes you *have to make* as you're learning how to love people. Mistakes are a necessary part of learning. I've heard you play the piano, and you do it beautifully. But when you were a child, didn't you make lots of mistakes while you were practicing?"

"Sure," said Sandra.

"And was it stupid of you to make those mistakes?"

Sandra finally smiled. "No. Everybody makes mistakes when they're learning to play."

"And everybody makes mistakes when they're learning to love people, too. Get the point? You don't feel loved enough yet to love other people consistently. Instead of feeling frustrated about it, just recognize that you made an unavoidable mistake. As you feel more loved, the things people do won't empty you out as easily as they do now. Eventually, you'll be able to keep loving Charles even when he's angry and more difficult to love."

In the beginning, we all need to feel the love of people who are willing to stay with us while we learn to tell the truth and feel their love. We need to be loved while we have nothing to give in return, and while we still use Getting and Protecting Behaviors. *Our partners need the same experience.* Are we willing sometimes to be the ones who give that to them? Are we willing to love a partner who gives us little or nothing in return? If not, we'll never learn to be loving and will give up the possibility of having loving relationships.

Sandra took the step of telling the truth about herself and experiencing unconditional love for herself before Charles even thought of doing such a thing. For quite some time, therefore, it was unavoidable that she had more love to give than Charles had. In virtually every relationship, one partner is farther along than the other in the process of feeling and giving love. Someone always has to take the first step. Sandra was willing to continue loving Charles despite the many times he had nothing to give her. That willingness is indispensable to the growth of a relationship.

Many people, however, refuse to give love when they're not immediately rewarded with something in return. They abandon their relationships whenever the exchange of love is "unfair." Such people cannot create loving relationships. Before a relationship can break out of a pattern of self-protection, and of trading Imitation Love, one partner must always be willing to tell the truth about himself and find unconditional love *without any promise of cooperation from the other*. He can then bring that love back to the relationship, which will unavoidably change as a result. But waiting for our partner to take the first step, or even to cooperate and take each step after us, is not only selfish, it's always unproductive.

In the last chapter, Charlotte wisely decided to do whatever it took to find Real Love for herself first, and *after* she did that, Darrell was motivated to do the same for himself. But Charlotte probably would never have seen an improvement in her relationship with Darrell if she'd insisted he take each step she took.

What if Darrell had *not* chosen to find Real Love? While it's true that, in some relationships, only one partner will ever take the steps toward finding Real Love and learning to be loving, it's also true that, in most cases, even those relationships will improve, because one partner will still feel more loved and will be much happier, even if the other partner doesn't change at all.

> We *learn* to love just like we learn anything else. It takes time and practice. Be patient with yourself as you make mistakes and learn. Be patient with others as they learn.

As we feel loved and learn to see and accept other people, we naturally become wise men and women for those who need to be seen and loved. Sometimes we're able to do that for only moments at a time, but those moments are very important both for us and for the people who are drowning. The more loved we feel, the longer and more frequently we are able to function as wise men.

Let me compare loving other people to sharing a bucket of water. When our bucket is empty—when we don't feel loved—we simply don't have anything to give anyone. Even when we want to love and help other people, we *can't*—there's nothing in the bucket to pour out. But when we do what it takes to get loved ourselves—as others pour what they have into *our* bucket—we can begin to share what we have, and the more we have, the more we have to give. When our bucket is full to overflowing, loving others becomes effortless.

However, there is something about loving other people that is different from pouring water from a bucket. As you share Real Love with those around you, you'll often find—at the end of the day, or at the conclusion of a single interaction—that you'll have more love than you started with, even if the person (or people) you loved gave you nothing in return. In some miraculous way, your bucket fills up as you empty it.

For that reason, I can't propose strongly enough that the fullest measure of happiness in life comes from sharing our love with others at every opportunity. We could sit back and wait for other people to love *us* and fill up our bucket to overflowing. Certainly we would then have love to share with others. But we can do much more. We can greatly accelerate the process of loving others by consciously choosing to love them *before* our own bucket is full. We can accept and forgive our partners, whatever their shortcomings. That is part of loving them. We need to eliminate anger from our lives. We also need to go beyond that whenever possible and comfort our partners when they're sad or angry, ask their forgiveness for

As you make conscious decisions to share your love with others, you'll experience a miraculous increase in the Real Love you *feel*, even if those whom you love don't return the love you give.

the mistakes we've made, perform random acts of kindness, and tell them we love them.

Sometimes, especially while you're still learning to love, you'll attempt to give more than you have. When that happens, your bucket will empty out, as Sandra's did with her husband. And then you can do what she did—call or visit someone who can fill your bucket back up. There's no limit to the amount of Real Love that's available to all of us. The more you practice loving people, the better you'll get at it, and the less likely you'll be to empty out.

The idea of loving the people around you may sound like a lot of work. But actually, once you feel sufficiently loved, it's natural that you'll care about the happiness of others. Giving Real Love is relatively effortless when compared with the enormous exertion associated with lying, attacking people, acting like a victim, and otherwise manipulating people. In fact, as you're learning how to love people, stress is a sign that you may not be unconditionally loving the people around you, and that you may need more Real Love for yourself.

We have many opportunities to love the people around us. If we use them, we'll create relationships and bring a happiness into our lives that we simply cannot imagine. The sooner we start, the more loving and happy we'll become.

Even after all we've discussed, many people still wonder how they can love someone they don't know very well or someone whose behavior is unacceptable. These doubts are variations of a central question: "If loving someone *because* he's handsome or smart or clever is a form of Imitation Love, why *do* we love another person?" Earlier in the chapter, I introduced you to Marilyn, who gave me an opportunity to consider this question. "There's something that's been bothering me," she said. "You say we can love everybody, but how can we love someone we don't know very well? Don't I have to know a lot about someone before I can really love that person?"

"Do you remember our first conversation?" I asked.

Marilyn smiled and said, "Yes, I do."

"Why did you smile?" I asked.

"Because it was wonderful. I really felt like you cared about me. It helped me understand how someone could unconditionally love another person."

"And how much did I know about you at the very beginning of that first conversation?"

She paused before answering. "Well, not very much, I guess."

"I didn't know anything about you. Does that answer your question about whether we have to know a lot about someone before we can love them?"

"Partly," she said. "So why *did* you care about me? I guess that's what I was really meaning to ask. If you didn't know anything about me, how could you really love me?"

"I loved you because you *needed* it. That's all the reason we ever need to love anyone—because he or she needs it. You're accustomed to people loving you because of some trait you have, but that's not really unconditional love, is it? When a child is born, what do we know about him? Nothing. We love that baby because he *needs* it. Why do we feed people who are starving? Because they're hungry. We don't need to know more than that. I didn't need to know anything about you to begin caring about your happiness. And you could feel that. Takes all the pressure off you to earn it, doesn't it?"

I explained to Marilyn that we can unconditionally *love* everyone just because they need it, but as we get to know people, it's natural that we *enjoy* being around some people more than others. Some people are more fun, more loving, and easier to be around than others, and it's understandable that we'd choose to spend a greater portion of our time with them.

Some people think that human beings are incapable of giving unconditional love. That's just not true. I've seen it more times than I can count. We *want* to care about the happiness of the people around us, and we fail to do that only because we get distracted by our own emptiness and fear, and by the Getting and Protecting Behaviors of others. But in the beginning—as we're learning—we give Real Love unevenly, intermittently, often mixed with Imitation Love. Sometimes we're capable of unconditionally caring about someone else's happiness, and at other times we react with Getting and Protecting Behaviors. Don't be discouraged when you do that. Keep practicing—you'll get much better at loving.

7

Playing a Beautiful Duet

The Joys of Mutually Loving Relationships

A mutually loving relationship—where each partner self-lessly cares about the happiness of the other—is the most delightful experience in the world. We all *want* that, but few of us are prepared to *be* the kind of truly loving partner that such a relationship requires. Before we can participate in a mutually loving relationship, we must learn to tell the truth about ourselves, feel unconditionally loved, and learn to love others. We can't play a duet until we first learn how to play an instrument by ourselves.

Telling the Truth About Ourselves

When we know our partner loves us no matter what mistakes we make or how we inconvenience him or her, why would we ever need to lie or otherwise protect ourselves from him? Elizabeth learned how easy it can be to tell the truth to a loving partner.

When Elizabeth came home from work, Henry immediately asked, "Did you make the bank deposit?"

"No, but I'll do it tomorrow," she answered.

Henry was obviously irritated. "You said you'd do it today."

Elizabeth paused before saying, "You're right. I did say that, but then I chose to do some other things I thought were more important. Looking at it now, I realize I made a mistake—I should have gone to the bank. It was selfish of me."

Henry's anger visibly decreased.

For most of their relationship, when Henry had expressed anger, Elizabeth had become afraid and protected herself. She'd claimed her mistakes were not her fault (lying). She'd acted hurt and offended (victim). Sometimes she'd expressed her anger at Henry (attacking) for not appreciating her, and occasionally she'd just walked off in tears (running, victim). Those Protecting Behaviors had made her feel safer for a moment, but they'd also made her feel even more distant from Henry and had severely affected their relationship.

In this interaction, however, Elizabeth employed none of her Protecting Behaviors. Instead, she applied several of the principles we've already discussed.

1. *She made a conscious decision to remember that Henry was loving her as well as he could.* She was able to do that only because, over the previous year, they had both taken the steps to find and share Real Love together. In the moment that Henry asked Elizabeth about the bank deposit, he was *not* being loving—he was attacking her with anger—but she was relatively filled with Real Love as a result of many *other* loving experiences with Henry *and* with other wise men and women. Without the distractions of emptiness and fear, we can see our partners clearly and remember

that their anger is nothing more than an indication that they're temporarily empty and afraid. We then have no need to protect ourselves and are able to tell the truth about our own behavior instead.

2. *She exercised* self-control *and made a conscious decision not to do anything to protect herself.* Even though Elizabeth felt relatively loved, Henry's attack was still somewhat threatening, and she did feel some need to defend herself. But she remembered how unproductive those behaviors had always been—that they had never made her truly happy or contributed to a loving relationship with anyone. As I've said before, there is a synergy between Real Love and self-control. If we wait for our behavior to change only as a result of the Real Love we receive, the progress can sometimes be slow. We also need to make conscious decisions to stop using Getting and Protecting Behaviors and to love other people.

3. *Elizabeth also made a deliberate choice to forgive her husband for attacking her and to be concerned for his happiness (Real Love).* That choice was much easier than it had been in the past because she felt loved herself, and because she remembered he was just empty, afraid, and protecting himself.

Mutually loving relationships develop only *after* many acts of faith. If you want such a relationship, you must be willing to tell the truth about yourself to your partner even on the many occasions when you're not sure he or she is being loving. In the beginning, you may be acting on pure faith, hoping there's a chance your partner might accept you. But you'll find it much easier to tell the truth about yourself to any partner if you already feel sufficiently filled with the acceptance and love of wise men and women to whom you have told the truth about yourself on other occasions. When you have that, it will be like money in the bank; you won't be afraid to tell the truth about yourself to your partner, because you won't *need* his or her acceptance in that given moment. Under those conditions, telling the truth becomes easy.

Telling the Truth About Our Partner

Although Henry was *less* angry after Elizabeth told the truth about herself, she could see that he was still unhappy. She remembered the many times she'd been happier after telling the truth about herself and feeling accepted, and she thought Henry might feel more loved and happy if he could tell the truth about his anger and feel her acceptance of him.

Although the general rule is that it's best to tell the truth about *ourselves,* occasionally we can help our partners by telling them the truth about *themselves.* When they feel empty and unloved, telling the truth about themselves is exactly what they need to do in order to feel seen and accepted. But when people are empty and afraid, they're occupied with desperately defending themselves, and at those times they're unlikely to see—much less be able to tell—the truth about themselves. So they may need someone to help them see the truth about their feelings and behavior. But just because someone has the *need* to hear the truth doesn't give us the *right* to speak it. Before we can even consider doing that, there are two important conditions that need to be met:

1. We need to be unconditionally loving. If we can't provide the unconditional acceptance people need while they hear the truth about themselves, we should be quiet. If we tell

other people the truth about themselves without Real Love, they will feel attacked, which will lead them to become more afraid and to use more Protecting Behaviors. If we ourselves are disappointed, angry, or afraid, we need to keep our opinions about other people to ourselves.

2. The person we're talking to needs to be capable of hearing what we're saying. Even if we feel loving, there are many times when other people are too afraid to hear what we have to say. If we push them too hard, they can only respond with Getting and Protecting Behaviors rather than feeling accepted and loved. And then we haven't helped them at all.

> ✒ Do not consider telling other people the truth about themselves unless you are unconditionally loving *and* they are feeling loved enough to hear what you are saying.

In a mutually loving relationship—where many unconditionally loving experiences have been shared in the past—our partner may feel safe enough for us to be able to help him or her tell the truth about himself. If we can do that, we're creating an opportunity for our partner to feel even more accepted and loved. That was Elizabeth's goal as she considered whether or not she should help Henry tell the truth about himself. Before she spoke, however, she honestly examined her feelings to be certain that she felt no anger or any need to be right. "You seem angry," she said.

Henry smiled as he sensed that Elizabeth was concerned about him, not accusing him of anything or trying to stop him from being angry.

"All day I work with people who don't understand me or care about me," said Henry. "When you didn't make the bank deposit, I thought you didn't care about me, either, and I protected myself by selfishly lashing out at you. Sometimes I forget that you love me."

"That's understandable. When I chose to do other things instead of making the bank deposit, I *was* selfish, and I wasn't caring about *you* as much as myself. And for years I made that kind of decision all the time."

They held each other and enjoyed the happiness that can only come from being honest, feeling loved, and loving someone else.

"It helped me a lot that you didn't defend yourself when I got angry," said Henry. "Thanks."

A potential confrontation was thus transformed into a loving experience. These miraculous interactions are common in mutually loving relationships—and we can all learn to have them.

You may have noticed that Elizabeth said exactly the same thing to Henry—"You seem angry"—that Michelle, whom we met in the previous chapter (p. 137), said to her husband when she tried to apply what she had learned in one of my seminars. But what a happier outcome! The difference is that Michelle tried—unintentionally—to bypass the entire process of feeling loved and learning how to love others, going straight to fixing her husband instead. She hadn't first learned how to tell the truth about herself and how to fill her own bucket with Real Love so that she'd have something to share with her husband. And so, when she tried to tell him the truth about himself, she was really manipulating him and protecting herself—and he felt that. The kind of relationship that Elizabeth had with Henry requires preparation—and it's worth it.

Telling the Truth All the Time

In a mutually loving relationship, partners are able to share what they think without fear of offending each other. It's delightful, as Elizabeth and Henry discovered more each day.

Elizabeth bought a new dress and put it on before going out to dinner with Henry. "Do you like my dress?" she asked.

Many of us feel trapped by questions like that. We're afraid of offending our partner and becoming the object of their disappointment or anger. In a mutually loving relationship, however, the answers are always easy.

Henry hugged Elizabeth and said, "I love you no matter what you wear."

Coming from someone who loves his partner, that is not a way of avoiding a potentially difficult question. When we feel loved and unconditionally love our partner, everything else—clothes, money, physical appearance, and so on—becomes insignificant.

On this occasion, however, Elizabeth really wanted an opinion about her dress. Although she felt loved by Henry, she was still a bit worried about what other people thought of her physical appearance. So she pressed the question. "I'm glad you love me," she said, "but I still want to know what you think of the dress. Would I look better in this or something else?"

"Well, actually, that's not my favorite dress. You look more attractive in some of the other clothes you wear," Henry admitted.

Because they had a mutually loving relationship, Elizabeth knew that his comment was about the *dress,* not *her*. She appreciated his opinion, and it helped her decide to take the dress back.

When two people know they're loved by one another, they

have what they've always wanted most. Anything else isn't worth getting anxious or offended about.

Making Requests

As I talk about unconditional love, it's understandable that many people become concerned. They worry that in the midst of all this unconditional acceptance of everything their partner does, they'll never get anything *they* want. When I describe the three choices in a relationship—live with it and like it, live with it and hate it, or leave it—some people protest, "So when do *my* needs get met? Do *I* never get to ask for anything?"

Yes, you do have a right to ask for what you want. In an unconditionally loving relationship, you can talk about anything. However, before you do that, there are a few points we need to discuss.

1. The need for Real Love

Before you get all excited and start presenting your partner with a list of the things you want—or the complaints you have—remember that genuine happiness comes from feeling unconditionally loved and loving other people. In the absence of Real Love, *anything* you push or manipulate your partner to give you (even subtly) will become a form of Imitation Love, and we already know the enormous disadvantages of consuming and trading Imitation Love.

Any time you think you need a particular thing from your partner, remind yourself that what you really need most is more Real Love in your life, and even *that* you can find from many sources—you don't have to get it from any one person in a given moment. Don't ruin the possibility of feeling Real Love by demanding *anything* from your partner. As you take the steps to find Real Love for yourself, two critical things will happen: First, you'll become genuinely happier. That's always more important than any of the individual *things* you might request from your partner. Second, without emptiness and fear, you'll be able to *ask* for what you want without using Getting and Protecting Behaviors. In short, when you're filled with Real Love as you make requests, your partner won't feel threatened, and you'll be happy no matter how he or she responds.

2. Requests versus expectations

If you remember the Law of Expectations from Chapter Three, you'll understand that you don't have the right to *expect* anything—certainly not love or happiness—from your partner. But you do have a right to make *requests* of your partner. Healthy requests can add to the happiness and strength of a relationship, while expectations and demands lead to disappointment and bitterness.

How do we tell the difference between a request and a demand, or a request and an expectation? By the presence or absence of *disappointment* and *anger*. We often make what we *call* requests, but they're not requests at all. The truth is revealed when we don't get what we "asked" for and are more than a little disappointed or even irritated, proving that we were really making a demand and having an expectation that our demand would be filled. When you make a true request

> In a loving relationship, you can always make a request, but when you're disappointed and angry if you don't get what you "requested," you demonstrate that you were really making a demand.

and it's denied, you won't feel more than a brief and superficial disappointment, and you'll never feel irritated.

As Elizabeth and Henry developed an increasingly loving relationship, they did more and more things together. Elizabeth usually did the household shopping by herself, but occasionally she asked Henry to go with her. He didn't particularly enjoy shopping, but sometimes he went along anyway. One evening, Elizabeth had to go to the grocery store, but she also wanted to spend some time with Henry, so she said, "I have to go to the grocery store. Would you like to go with me?"

"No," he responded. "I'm feeling pretty lazy. I'd rather stay home."

Elizabeth did feel a moment of disappointment when Henry said he wasn't going with her. She'd hoped to have the pleasure of his company—otherwise she wouldn't have asked. The feeling lasted only for a moment, however, and she was not disappointed in *Henry* or in their *relationship*. She remembered that she was loved—by Henry and by others. When people are certain they're loved, they have what matters most and don't have the need to insist that their individual demands be met from moment to moment.

Unconditional love really does make us happier than anything else can, and when we have enough of that, we can easily bear being deprived of other things. As we feel sufficient Real Love in our lives, we can eventually make requests of our partners and feel no disappointment at all when, from time to time, we don't get what we ask for. Feeling loved truly is like twenty million dollars in the bank.

3. Clear requests

You'll significantly enhance the likelihood of receiving what you want if you state your requests clearly. Don't throw out vague hints, and don't expect your partner to read your mind. Elizabeth learned how to make clear requests of Henry.

Early in the process of their learning to love each other, Elizabeth and Henry made a lot of mistakes, and sometimes they needed help. On one occasion, they talked to a wise friend about a problem they were having. "I told Henry more than a week ago that I'd be working in the vegetable garden this Saturday," Elizabeth said, "and I mentioned that it would need some tilling. Then on Saturday I went out there and worked for more than four hours. I kept waiting for him to come out and help, but he never showed up. And he wonders why I'm mad about it."

Henry shrugged his shoulders and lifted his eyebrows in a gesture of helpless ignorance. "I didn't *know* you were out there waiting for me," he protested.

"But you saw me leaving the house with my work clothes on."

They began to argue about the details of who saw and did what.

The wise man finally interrupted. "Elizabeth, you wanted Henry to work with you in the vegetable garden Saturday because you needed help with the tiller. Is that right?"

"Yes."

"Did you ever say to him, 'Henry, I would like you to help me run the tiller in the vegetable garden on Saturday at a specific time'?"

There was a lengthy pause before Elizabeth responded. "Well, I told him I'd be working out there on Saturday, and that the garden needed tilling."

Elizabeth had given Henry a bunch of *hints* about helping her, but she'd never made a single clear request. We tend to avoid making direct requests for two reasons: First, it's what we were trained to do by the people around us as they did the same thing with *us*. It was their unconscious way of getting us to prove we cared enough about them to respond to their un-voiced expectations. Second, by dropping hints we avoid the possibility of having someone actually *refuse* us directly. We don't like being refused. It makes us feel rejected and unloved.

"I know you think you gave Henry enough information to get him out to the garden," said the wise man, "and if he were perfectly sensitive, he might have caught on to all those hints and showed up. But you don't have the right to expect Henry to read your mind. If you want something from him, you have to clearly tell him what you want. And of course, you have to be prepared for him to say no. Otherwise, you're not really making a request—you're issuing a demand."

If we make vague requests, or if we drop nebulous hints here and there, we shouldn't be surprised when we don't get what we want. Be clear about telling your partner what you want. Be certain you feel loved and loving when you make your requests. And then remember that your partner does not *have* to agree to your requests in order to express his or her love for you.

4. *Requests and promises*

I've talked several times about the disadvantages of expecta-tions in relationships. But in Chapter Three, I also talked about promises. When you make a request, and your partner agrees to it, he or she has made a promise. You then have a right to expect your partner to fulfill that promise. However, loving relationships are not built on promises; they're built on Real Love. Although you have a *right* to expect that a promise will be kept, you'd be foolish to ruin your happiness or your relationship by holding that expectation over your partner's head, or worse, by becoming angry when he or she fails to meet it. Don't make the awful mistake of beating your partner with a promise he's made. My wife, Donna, has demonstrated how to respond wisely to a partner when he or she breaks a promise.

We'd invited several friends to dinner, and she had planned to be out of the house doing errands for several hours before the time of their arrival. Before she left, she asked me to perform several tasks that needed to be done in her absence—cut up some carrots, straighten up and vacuum some rooms, move a load of laundry from the washer to the dryer—and I agreed.

Three hours later, when the door opened and she walked back in, I realized immediately that I'd completely forgotten to do everything I'd promised. Instead of vacuuming the floors immediately and setting a timer to remind myself of the other jobs, I'd selfishly become involved in my own concerns and let her down. She walked right up to me, smiled, and said, "You didn't do any of those jobs, did you?"

I winced and said, "No."

Without a hint of disappointment in her voice, she asked, "Do you think you can get it all done before the guests arrive?" There was no doubt whose responsibility it was to correct this mistake.

"It will be close," I said, "but I think so."

"I need you to cut up the carrots first," she said. "Cooking is the next thing I have to do."

Even when our partners do make promises, we'd be wise to keep our expectations to a minimum, because expectations so often lead to disappointment and anger. And when your partner does fail to keep a promise, the only productive response is to love him or her unconditionally and simply tell him the truth about the mistake he made, as Donna did with me. In a mutually loving relationship, there is never any place for disappointment or anger. Without expectations, everything we receive becomes a *gift,* rather than the filling of an order. You don't want a relationship based on promises and expectations; you want a relationship based on gifts and Real Love.

5. No keeping score

When we make genuine requests—without expectations— we don't keep track of when we get what we want and when we don't. We don't compare the number of requests we've made to the number our partner has made. We don't keep score. This principle should be obvious if we understand that true requests are made without expectations, but people are so used to keeping score in their relationships that I think the point bears repeating. We *cannot* be happy if we keep score with our partners.

6. Living with it and liking it

As we make loving requests, we make the first of the three choices described in Chapter Three as being available to us in relationships: living with it and liking it. We do not try to change our partners. We accept them as they are, and we *ask* them if they are willing to give us something we want. If they refuse, we accept that and continue to love them.

———

You do not have to wait until both you and your partner are unconditionally loving before you make a request of your partner. If that were the case, most people would have to wait a very long time before making their first request. What I do suggest, however, is that requests are generally not useful until a minimum of two requirements is satisfied: First, *you* must be *loving* enough to make your request without Getting and Protecting Behaviors (which include disappointment and anger). And second, although your partner may not be capable of being *loving,* he or she must at least *feel loved* enough to hear your request without protecting himself. If your partner is sufficiently empty and afraid at the time you make your request, he or she can only perceive it as threatening—even if you deliver it in a loving way—and so you would be foolish to make it. Because no request can ever bring you the happiness you'll get from receiving and giving Real Love, you should never do anything that would interfere with feeling loved and loving others.

> Before you make a request, be certain that you feel unconditionally loving and that your partner feels loved enough to hear your request without feeling threatened.

Working Things Out

One evening, Elizabeth came into the room where Henry was watching a basketball game. She didn't enjoy watching sports and had been looking forward to watching a movie after a long day at work.

In the past, when Henry and Elizabeth didn't have a mutually loving relationship, Elizabeth had felt trapped and angry when Henry was watching something on television that she didn't enjoy. She thought it meant Henry didn't care about her, and most of the time she was right. She would then criticize him angrily (attacking) for not caring about her, whine about how he never considered what she wanted (victim), or leave the room and sulk for hours (running). Every little thing—watching television, spending money, disagreeing about the children, among other things—would become a huge source of contention between them. That's because, without Real Love, every crumb of Imitation Love becomes very important, and we feel compelled to grab it and protect it.

On this occasion, however, Elizabeth felt loved and happy. She and Henry had been practicing telling the truth and loving each other for some time. "How much longer will the game last?" asked Elizabeth.

Most of the time, when people ask a question like that, they're launching an indirect attack. What they really mean to say is: "I can't believe you're watching television again. And of course you're watching something I hate. How much longer are you going to sit there, keeping me from watching what I want?" But Elizabeth had no such hidden agenda. She was simply gathering information that could influence her next question or decision. That's what real questions are for.

"They haven't been playing long," said Henry, "so it will probably go for another two hours or so."

"I was interested in watching a movie," said Elizabeth, "but if the basketball game is important to you, I'll do something else."

"I'm enjoying the game, but it's not a big deal. I wouldn't mind watching a movie."

With minimal effort, they chose a movie they could both enjoy.

Henry did not "give in." Because he felt loved, he knew he didn't have to change what he was doing to make Elizabeth happy. He didn't feel pressured into giving her something she wanted. Rather, he made a conscious decision to do something loving for her. If the basketball game had been sufficiently important to him, he'd have said so, and Elizabeth would have done something else. In fact, a week later, that's exactly what happened.

"How much longer will that game last?" asked Elizabeth.

"Probably an hour or so," answered Henry. "I'd really like

to see who wins. Is there something you wanted to see after that?"

"Yes, will you let me know when you're done?"

"Sure."

Elizabeth was slightly inconvenienced by Henry's choice, but because she felt loved, she wasn't the least bit disappointed or angry. In loving relationships, we don't have to give our partners everything they want. What we do give on each occasion should be a *gift*, freely offered, and the most important gift of all is our unconditional acceptance and love. When our partners feel loved, they don't require us to give them every little thing they want.

In every relationship, there will always be conflicts about specific interests, preferences, and schedules. But when two people care about each other's happiness, those conflicts are easily resolved, as Elizabeth and Henry have demonstrated. We'll talk more about conflict resolution in Chapter Nine.

Faith in Mutual Love

Nathan and Dena had practiced telling the truth and loving each other for years when, on Dena's birthday, her friend Julie called and asked, "What did Nathan give you for your birthday?"

"Nothing," Dena answered.

"How disappointing!" said Julie. "Did he forget about it?"

Dena laughed. "No, he didn't forget. Nathan is my best friend in the world. Every day he tells me he loves me—with his words and with the things he does. He smiles and touches me whenever he sees me. He accepts and loves me no matter what I do. How could I want more than that for my birthday?"

Dena and Nathan had developed a relationship so loving

that Nathan didn't constantly have to prove his love to Dena, even on her birthday. And because Dena chose to remember and trust their many loving experiences together, she saw the evidence of his love everywhere, instead of seeing every little mistake or omission as a sign that he didn't care about her. She had faith that Nathan was doing his best to love her, even on those occasions when he paid her little attention or actually became irritated with her. With that attitude, she felt loved all the time.

It's unfortunate that most people give birthday and Christmas gifts at least in part because they feel they have to prove their affection to their partners. And they're afraid of the consequences of not giving a gift. That sense of obligation is not compatible with Real Love.

Becoming One

In a mutually loving relationship, the partners become one. They're united in their desire to contribute to each other's happiness. There is no trading, competition, manipulation, or sense of obligation. Each partner fills the needs of the other because he or she wants to. Loving people don't do this so their partner will be grateful, nor do they serve each other to avoid their partner's displeasure.

8

Real Love in All
Our Relationships

Spouses, Children, Friends, and Co-workers

The principles we've discussed thus far have important applications in every aspect of our lives. They change our relationships with our spouses, children, other family members, co-workers, and even God.

The Truth About Marriage

Half the marriages in this country end in divorce, and most partners who stay married are not experiencing the joy of an unconditionally loving relationship. They simply avoid major conflict and call that happiness. Clearly, most of us are misguided about what marriage is and how it works.

Without unconditional love, we desperately gather every scrap of praise, power, pleasure, and safety we can get. When we find someone—or think we have—who gives us those things consistently, we develop a powerful hope that he or she will continue to do that and make us happy. And when our anticipation of getting Imitation Love from a specific person is great enough, we call that feeling falling in love. We tend to fall in love with someone because that person makes *us* feel good. That is not Real Love.

After falling in love, we naturally want to guarantee a consistent supply of what we believe to be happiness. And *that* is almost always why we get married—to ensure that someone will be there every day to make us happy.

We're not being entirely selfish. We do have *some* concern for the happiness of our spouse. But without feeling unconditionally loved ourselves, we can only be empty and afraid, and in that condition our *primary* motivation for getting married is selfish. When we're starving to death ourselves, it's very difficult to be concerned primarily about the needs of anyone else. Many of us deny the selfishness in our marriage, but we prove it every time we're disappointed and irritated when our partner fails to give us what we want.

When two people get married, they exchange promises that boil down to this: "I will always love you more than I love anyone else." That's what each partner *says,* but each person *hears* the other say much more:

> "I promise to make you happy—always. I will heal your past wounds and satisfy your present needs and expectations—even when you don't express them. I will lift you up when you're discouraged. I will accept and love you no matter what mistakes you make. I give to you all that I have or ever will have. And I will never leave you."

Neither partner is consciously aware of making these many promises, but each partner still hears them and insists that they be fulfilled. Lacking unconditional love, many couples constantly struggle with the impossible task of trying to make one another happy. Disappointment and anger are then guaranteed, no matter how hard they try.

From the beginning, most marriages are fatally burdened with the impossible expectations each partner places on the other to make him or her happy.

When we feel empty and unloved, we understandably expect the people around us—especially those who claim to love us—to give us what we want and make us feel better. In the case of a spouse, where marriage commitments have been exchanged, we feel especially justified in having those expectations. But even in marriage expectations are usually selfish, because the Law of Choice still applies. Bruce learned about the Law of Choice when he complained to me about his wife, Paula.

After listening for several minutes, I said, "You seem pretty angry at Paula."

"Of course I am," said Bruce. "Who wouldn't be? I do a lot for her, and all she does is complain. This isn't a marriage anymore. We haven't even had sex for months."

"*I* haven't had sex with Paula for all those months, either," I said, "but *I'm* not angry at her."

Bruce looked rather surprised. "But that's different! She's my wife!"

"So what?"

"But she's *supposed* to have sex with me. We're married!"

"You believe that because you're married to Paula, she's *obligated* to have sex with you—how much fun do you think that is for her? How would *you* like to be with someone who *forced* you to be with them and do things for them? You can't have a loving relationship with Paula as long as you keep demanding things from her—and I don't mean just sex, I mean *anything*."

I then talked to Bruce about expectations, the Law of Choice, Getting and Protecting Behaviors, and unconditional love.

Most of us get married so we can feel justified in demanding that our partner make us happy. When he or she doesn't do that, we just insist more urgently, which begins a pattern of mutual manipulation or outright resistance but certainly doesn't produce the Real Love we want. As long as we use marriage as a whip to force our spouse to give us what we want, we'll never be happy.

———

So what *is* marriage? *Marriage is a commitment* we make to stay with our partner while *we* learn to unconditionally love *him* or *her*. It's an agreement to stay in a relationship for a lifetime, even when our partner isn't loving. It's also a commitment to limit the sharing of some things (living together, sex, financial resources, and so on) to one partner.

That may not be a romantic definition of marriage—and I realize it may not be a universally accepted one—but it is clear and useful, which I'll demonstrate as I respond to a couple of the questions that invariably arise when people hear that definition. For example, many people wonder, "Since almost all partners are not unconditionally loving, why in the world would I *want* to get married in the first place and make a commitment to share my body, my financial resources, and so on with only one person? And why would I want to make such a commitment for a lifetime? It doesn't sound like marriage is such a great idea."

If we view marriage as an opportunity to squeeze Imitation Love out of another person, it usually *doesn't* turn out very well, and a commitment to trade what you have to offer with only one person would indeed be a questionable decision. But when we see marriage as an opportunity to learn to love another person unconditionally, it becomes a different experience entirely. With that perspective, the sex, praise, financial resources, and everything else we have to share become tools with which we express our affection for our partner. When we reserve some of those tools exclusively for one partner, we're able to achieve a more profound level of loving with that person.

Imagine, for example, how you would feel if you knew I had prepared a delicious dessert for you and walked clear across town to deliver it to you. On the way, I was approached by several friends, some of them dear to me, asking for a portion of the dessert. In fact, I was also approached by others I didn't even know, who offered me money for the delicacy, but I refused them all, reserving the prize for you. Knowing that, would my delicacy not taste all the sweeter? More important, would you not feel loved and would our relationship not therefore be enriched?

That's how our partner feels if we save our sexual activity until we get married. Sex becomes an extraspecial gift, like the dessert, instead of something we've casually shared with dozens of others. It becomes an opportunity to express a deeper, more powerful level of affection, and our partner can feel that—as do we when we are the exclusive recipient of our partner's sexual attentions. Of course, that feeling continues when we keep being sexually faithful after marriage. I am not trying to dictate anyone's behavior, only suggesting that when we are sexually exclusive, we multiply the possibilities that our partner will feel loved. That alone is more than enough reason to consider being sexually faithful to one partner. We'll discuss an additional reason to be sexually faithful before marriage in a following section.

Moreover, as we exclusively, or predominantly, devote other resources in our lives—finances, companionship, service, living together—to one partner, he or she will also feel more loved. I re-emphasize that as we freely offer these things, they become gifts, and we create opportunities for our partners to receive them as evidence of our unconditional love.

But let's be practical. Sometimes in a marriage the things we want are not freely offered. Bruce and Paula discovered that in their relationship.

One evening Paula got home late. She'd worked all day and had dropped by to see her mother, who was disabled and often needed help around the house. When Paula walked in the door, she discovered that their two teenagers were watching television, they hadn't done any homework, and no one had done anything about dinner. She was angry when she talked to Bruce. "What have *you* been doing?" she asked.

Of course, Bruce didn't think he'd done anything wrong, and he was offended. They exchanged Getting and Protecting Behaviors, which is always a mistake.

Bruce later talked to me about their unpleasant conversation, looking for a little sympathy, and I suggested that he might be failing to take advantage of the many opportunities available to him to learn to love his wife.

"What?" he said. Bruce had not anticipated the conversation would go in that direction.

"Do you want to have an incredible, richly fulfilling marriage with Paula, or do you want to keep complaining about what you've got? A or B?"

He decided he wanted a richly fulfilling relationship, so I suggested the only way to accomplish that was for him to learn to love Paula unconditionally. "That means to care about her happiness," I reminded him. "If you consistently remember that simple phrase, you'll know what to do most of the time." But then I helped him see specifically what he could have done differently the night she was angry at him. She'd called him on the cell phone to tell him she'd be late. He knew what needed to be done without being told like a child. He could have fixed dinner or gone out to get some. He could have instructed the children to get their homework done. He could have thought about her needs and offered his service as a gift.

Couples in a marriage have a delightful opportunity to promise each other over long periods of time to relieve each other's burdens and provide loving acts of kindness in ways that are seldom seen in other relationships. Bruce gradually realized he was being selfish, learned to tell the truth about himself, and began to feel unconditionally loved. He and Paula made clear agreements about who was responsible from week to week for certain duties, such as preparing meals, picking up children, taking care of Paula's mother, and so on. It's much more effective to do that—make agreements about doing things long-term—than to wonder from day to day who's going to do what and when. Clear agreements prevent a lot of disagreements and unhappiness.

When Real Love is involved, expectations can actually be healthy—despite all the terrible things I've previously said about them. As Paula drove home from work on yet another evening, she realized that she *expected* the house would be in order, a meal ready, and the kids' homework started. She and Bruce had arranged all those things days beforehand, and she felt *loved* because she knew Bruce wanted to do them for her. Even though she had expectations about those tasks being done, she still felt loved because he'd *freely offered* those gifts. Sometimes Bruce *didn't* accomplish the things he promised, but because she knew he was *trying* to love her, and because she had faith that he was doing his best, she didn't become too disappointed, and she didn't become angry. Paula's expectations actually helped her to feel more loved.

It's wonderful when your spouse freely offers what you need, as Bruce finally learned to do. But what if he or she doesn't do that? Then you must first learn to feel loved yourself and learn to make loving requests, as we discussed in Chapter Seven. Ask your spouse to make commitments to take responsibility for regular duties, as Bruce and Paula did. Marriage is a *partnership*. Things do have to get done— money made, meals prepared, children raised, errands run, and so on. But always remember that nothing positive will happen if you push for any change while you're not being loving yourself. No *thing* you want from your partner is as important as the infusion of Real Love into your relationship.

And if your partner says no to most or all of your requests? Remember that marriage is a *lifetime* commitment to learn to love your partner. Don't give up on this process too quickly. Keep filling your own life with Real Love. Keep learning to love and serve your partner. Keep making your loving requests. I *know* that can often be very difficult, but the potential rewards are without equal.

———

Viewing marriage as a lifetime commitment helps us to persist in the process of learning to love our partner. A friend of mine once came to me and said, "I want a divorce."

"Why?" I asked.

"I'm miserable. My wife just doesn't understand me. She—"

I'd heard this list of complaints before, so I gently interrupted. "Your wife is not the cause of your unhappiness. You felt unloved and empty long before you met her. And then you expected her to make you happy, but she couldn't do that because she'd never been unconditionally loved, either. She didn't make you unhappy. She just couldn't fulfill your expectations that she would change your whole life."

My friend sighed. He knew that what I was saying was true. I continued. "When you married your wife, you made a commitment to continue your relationship even when it became difficult. You have an important opportunity here to learn how to love her—and how to love other people. If you leave her now, you'll learn nothing and you'll just repeat the same mistakes in your next relationship."

———

Without the commitment of marriage, we tend to leave relationships whenever we're uncomfortable. And then we don't learn how to be loving. However, some people, like Alice, do understand the principle of commitment in marriage.

Alice's husband was quite unloving, but she had learned to tell the truth about herself and felt accepted and loved by several wise friends. For several years, she'd tried to share that love with her husband, but he remained afraid, angry, and alone. A wise friend asked Alice, "Why do you stay married to him?"

"You stayed with *me* while I learned to tell the truth and feel loved," said Alice. "When I married my husband, I promised to do the same for *him*."

It's easy to love someone who loves us in return. But when Alice chose to continue loving someone who didn't love her, she learned a great deal about Real Love.

> Marriage is not an opportunity to dump our expectations for happiness on our partner—it's a *commitment* we make to stay with our partner while *we* learn to love *him* or *her* unconditionally.

When I talk about the lifelong commitment of marriage, I am not saying there's never a reason to dissolve a marriage, but we'll talk more about leaving in Chapter Nine.

Exclusive Relationships

An exclusive relationship is one in which each partner agrees to make the other the primary focus of his or her attention. Marriage is an example. But despite what we've been taught from childhood, an exclusive relationship is not required for happiness. We don't *have* to "go steady" or have a lover or be married in order to be really happy.

A mutually loving relationship naturally develops between any two people who feel unconditionally loved. It doesn't have to be exclusive. We can have that kind of relationship with many friends or family members. In fact, divorced, widowed, and single people with several mutually loving relationships are far happier than married couples or lovers who have an exclusive relationship without Real Love as its foundation.

Nevertheless, after two people have promised each other to make their relationship exclusive, they each have a right to expect those promises to be kept. Blake discovered the significance of his promise in a conversation with Sylvia.

Blake and Sylvia had been married for eight years, and during most of that time Sylvia had been accusing Blake of flirting with beautiful women. Blake denied it and was irritated whenever she brought it up. Sylvia talked about her problem one day when they were at the home of a wise friend whom they'd known for many years.

"I want to ask you about something," Sylvia said to their friend. "Blake is always flirting with other women, and I don't like it."

"I do not," Blake said in a huff.

"I'm guessing, Blake," said the wise man, "that she's not making this up out of thin air. You must be doing *something* to make her think you're flirting with other women. So just for a minute, let's listen to what she has to say. We've got nothing to lose. Okay?"

Blake shrugged his shoulders as he made a decision to trust his friend. Although he didn't refer to them by name, the wise man was following the First and Second Rules of Seeing, which we discussed in Chapter Four. Sylvia had spoken first, so she was the speaker in this conversation.

"Whenever we go out," Sylvia said, "he's always looking at other women—the pretty ones, of course. When we're at a party, you can always find him talking to some beautiful single woman, and he always has his hands on her, touching her hands, her arms, her shoulders, her waist, her back. It makes me so mad I could scream. And then when I try to talk to him about it, he says it was nothing. He must think I'm stupid or something. Do you see what I'm talking about?"

"Blake, do you understand what she's saying?" asked the wise man.

"I don't look at other women all that much, and when we're at parties, I hardly touch 'em at all. It's not like we're sneaking off together. It's just not that big a deal."

"Blake," said the wise man, "remember that we've been friends for a long time. I'm only telling you this because I care about the relationship you have with Sylvia. When you got married, you promised to be completely faithful to her sexually—completely, not fifty percent or ninety percent or even ninety-nine percent. When you go out in public and look at other women, you're telling her that your sexual attention is wandering. There's no other way to interpret that. You're violating your promise to Sylvia. Do you see that?"

Blake looked thoughtful as his friend continued. "And when you touch other women, you continue to be unfaithful sexually. You may justify yourself and say that it has nothing to do with sex, but when *you and I talk,* do you ever touch *my* hands or arms or shoulders or waist in the tender way that you touch those women's? *Not a chance.* It's about sex, and Sylvia knows that you're violating the promise you made to her. Again, I'm not trying to make you feel bad, only helping you see how you're hurting your relationship."

When he realized his friend was right, Blake began to see the significance of what he'd been doing, and he changed his behavior.

As we keep the promises we make in an exclusive relationship, we communicate to our partner that we care about his or her happiness, and that nonverbal caring will contribute to the strength of our relationship. Violating those promises can obviously be very destructive.

Sex in Relationships

We're surrounded by references to sex—in books, movies, magazines, calendars, and newspapers; on television, the radio, and billboards, as well as in the jokes and stories we tell each other. The depiction of sexual desire and activity— sometimes subtle, but often quite graphic—has become so common that we accept it as normal. Sex is portrayed as a healthy appetite to be gratified as casually as eating a meal. We admire and envy sexually attractive men and women, and we're convinced that if we're sexually appealing ourselves, we'll feel worthwhile and happy.

Although sex can be a healthy addition to a relationship that's based on Real Love, it can also become a powerful source of Imitation Love. In the absence of Real Love, we desperately want to be valued for *something,* and we settle for earning the praise and admiration of other people. When someone finds us sexually attractive, we feel acceptable, important, and even lovable.

Brenda was fifteen years old, and although her parents did their best, they had no idea how to love her unconditionally. As a result, she felt insignificant and alone. But there was one bright spot in her life. Ryan, a sixteen-year-old boy at school, thought Brenda was beautiful, and he communicated that whenever he looked at her and talked to her. It was more positive attention than she'd ever received, and for the first time she could remember, she felt worthwhile.

Ryan, however, was not primarily concerned for Brenda's happiness. He liked how *he* felt when she looked at him, talked to him, and allowed him to touch her. When Ryan's expressions of affection became increasingly sexual, Brenda cooperated without hesitation because he made her feel important, and she was willing to do anything to maintain that feeling. Not surprisingly, she ignored her parents and others when they warned her about the dangers inherent in her behavior.

Eventually, when the thrill of using Brenda faded, Ryan abandoned her to find entertainment somewhere else. Brenda was briefly devastated, of course, but she also learned from this experience a pattern of behavior that would bring her pleasure all her life. She discovered that if boys and men found her sexually appealing, they would praise her and "love" her, which felt a great deal better than being ignored or criticized. Sexual attraction is a very important criterion for most of us as we choose partners, and not just in marriage. Which of us chooses to seek out a stimulating conversation with the least physically attractive man or woman at a social gathering? Without thinking about it, we treat physically "ugly" people differently from the way we treat those who are obviously beautiful. Put a gorgeous model and an overweight, "unattractive" woman in any group of people and see if the two women are treated equally—by either the men or the women. Unthinkable.

This emphasis on physical attraction is everywhere. When a friend introduces his or her child to us for the first time, we feel obligated to say something about the child's *appearance,* don't we? Even in the bedtime stories we tell our children, the princess is always beautiful and the prince is handsome. At an early age, our children learn that beautiful people consistently get more attention and "love" than those who are plain. So our children work to be physically attractive, and if they don't succeed, they believe they're defective. Why else would anorexia and bulimia be epidemic among young women? Physical appearance affects virtually every relationship we have.

Many of us deny that our fixation on physical appearance has anything to do with sex. "There's nothing wrong with enjoying physical beauty," we say. "It's like admiring a great work of art, or a piece of literature, or an exceptional skill." Ridiculous. Do we really prefer one nose or pair of lips over another because it conforms to some *mathematical* model? Do we admire long, wavy hair because it's more *functional* than a balding scalp? Do we enjoy large breasts because they're *artistically* more pleasing than a flat chest? No. We need to admit that most of us are attracted—however unconsciously—to physical characteristics that are *sexually* appealing. Models are not chosen for magazine covers and billboards because of their intellectual superiority—and we pay them very well for the feelings they arouse in us.

If we care unconditionally about the happiness of another person, why would our love be affected *in any way* by that person's physical appearance? Why would we care more about the happiness of a beautiful woman—or man—than an "ugly" one? We wouldn't. So the fact that we really are more attracted to physically beautiful and sexually attractive people proves that we often do not love our partners unconditionally.

———

As we discussed in Chapter Two, in addition to the praise we get from sex, we get other forms of Imitation Love as well. When Brenda attracted men to her with her sexual desirability and availability, she discovered that she had considerable *power* over their behavior. Although she was powerless with her parents and most other people, Brenda discovered that with sex she could persuade men to do almost anything. If we can't have what we want most—Real Love—the power to control other people is intoxicating. In return for that power, Brenda gave them *pleasure*. The physical pleasures of sex—sight, sound, touch, taste, and smell—are intense. When our lives are otherwise unfulfilling, sex provides an immediate thrill so powerful that we're often willing to risk serious social, emotional, health, and even criminal consequences to get it. Many relationships are initially based on an exchange of the praise, power, and pleasure derived from sex.

> In the absence of Real Love, sex can become a powerful and dangerous source of Imitation Love, and many of us will do almost anything to get it.

Like all pursuits that replace Real Love, sex can become a seductive danger. In the ancient Greek epic, *The Odyssey*, Odysseus struggled mightily to return home to his family, and in the process he was required to overcome great trials placed in his path by jealous and angry gods. At one point in the journey, his ship passed an island where the Sirens lived. These mysterious bird-women produced a song so beautiful that sailors were completely bewitched. Mindless of the danger, they followed the captivating sound and drove their ships onto the rocks at the edge of the island.

Sex can be like the song of the Sirens. People without Real Love are powerfully attracted to it, and as they pursue it, they lose their direction, fatally distracted from their journey toward real happiness. And then they break up on the rocks of Imitation Love, destroyed by emptiness, disappointment, and misery.

Real Love is the only thing that will ever make us genuinely happy; therefore, anything that distracts us from telling the truth and finding Real Love is emotionally and spiritually deadly. *That* is the potential danger of sex—that it can *distract* us from finding unconditional love. In the absence of Real Love, sex is so enjoyable that when we get enough of it, we think we're truly happy.

To make a practical analogy, imagine that you and I start work at a company on the same day, and we've never known each other before. As we become friends, I begin to give you a hundred dollars every time I see you in the hall. Of course, it wouldn't take long before you'd start creating opportunities to meet me in the hall, but both of us would inevitably begin to wonder—as you smiled at me each time—whether you were interested in *me,* for who I am, or in my money. Similarly, if you experience the pleasures of sex with someone early in a relationship—before you really know that person, before you've shared the truth about yourself, and before you've made an exclusive commitment to one another—you can't help becoming hopelessly confused. You lose your sense of what's true and what's real. You cannot know whether you care about your partner's happiness or whether you simply enjoy the way he or she pleases you sexually.

Many of us cannot feel worthwhile unless we're involved in

> If you have sex with someone early in a relationship, you can't know whether you care about your partner's happiness or whether you simply enjoy the way he or she pleases you sexually.

a sexual relationship. Our society actually views people as defective if they don't have a sexual partner. In fact, many of us are so obsessed with finding sexual satisfaction that when we can't have a satisfying sexual relationship with a real person, we turn to fantasies fueled by the pictures in magazines, videotapes, on the Internet, and so on. The unspeakably large pornography industry—which includes many mainstream and socially acceptable motion pictures—just proves the extent of our addiction to sex as a substitute for Real Love and genuine happiness. Sexual pleasure is advertised everywhere as the ultimate thrill and evidence of success and self-worth. But tragically, *without Real Love*, sex will only lead us away from feeling unconditionally loved and from sharing that love with others—and that's in addition to the obvious health and social liabilities of sexually transmitted diseases and unwanted children.

As I speak of a possible solution to the potential dangers of sex, I'm not interested in imposing a moral code on anyone. I'm interested only in offering a way to minimize the profound unhappiness that is uniformly experienced by those who use sex as a form of Imitation Love.

The solution I suggest is twofold: First, we need to fill our lives with Real Love. Without emptiness and fear, we will no longer have a need to fill ourselves in an obsessive way with the hollow pleasures of sex and other forms of Imitation

Love. I've counseled many self-acknowledged sex addicts and others who have used sex as a way to fill the emptiness in their lives, and I can state from experience that as they have felt the effects of Real Love, they've gradually lost their desire to use sex in an unhealthy way, even though, in many cases, they'd already tried unsuccessfully to use self-control and had even been in therapy to change their behavior, with equally unsuccessful results. That's because when we're filled with Real Love, sex becomes an *expression* of love, rather than a substitute for it.

Second, I suggest that we limit sexual activity to long-term committed relationships, i.e., marriage. For thousands of years, societies all over the world have prescribed marriage to prevent the destructive effects of indiscriminate sex. Earlier in the chapter, we discussed one reason to save sex for marriage—to provide a special expression of affection for your partner. In the following story we see how Steven, a single man, learned about another benefit of saving sex for marriage. If you're already married, you need to fill your life with Real Love and try to use that as the motivation for the sexual experiences you share with your spouse. The two stories following Steven's will illustrate the effect of Real Love on sex in marriage.

Steven had dated many women, and he talked about one of them to his wise friend. "I've been dating a woman for two months," he said, "and I think I love her. But I'm not sure if it's unconditional love. How can I know?"

"Are you having sex with her?" asked the wise man.

"Yes."

"Then it's almost impossible for you to know if it's Real Love. While you're enjoying the enormous praise, power, and pleasure of having sex with this woman, it will be very difficult for you to determine whether you genuinely care about *her* happiness—which is Real Love—or whether you just like how she makes *you* feel—which is Imitation Love. Have you had sex with other women?"

"Sure," said Steven.

"And in the beginning of those relationships, did you think you loved them?"

Steven smiled. "Yes, sometimes, and I think I get the point you're making."

"How did those relationships turn out?"

"Obviously, they didn't last, because I don't associate with any of those women anymore. While I was having sex with them, we had a lot of fun, and several times I really thought it might be love. But when the excitement of the sex wore off, we didn't have much of a relationship left."

Steven stopped having sex with his girlfriend and soon discovered that he didn't really care about her happiness. He learned that he was still too selfish to love anyone unconditionally. Sobered by that discovery, he began the process of telling the truth about himself and finding Real Love.

When two people care about each other's happiness in a committed, exclusive relationship—marriage—physical intimacy becomes a natural expression of love and great fun.

Earlier in this chapter, we met Bruce and his wife, Paula, both of whom were unhappy with the sexual part of their marriage. But then Bruce learned how to tell the truth about himself, feel loved, and care about Paula's happiness. When Paula felt Bruce's concern for her, that changed their relationship considerably as she began to feel enormously attracted to him, both emotionally and physically. They began to enjoy sex regularly, and it became a more fulfilling experience than anything they'd ever known.

After a while, Bruce said to me, "I don't even know what word to use for what we used to do, because having sex now is a completely different experience from what it was."

For ages, men have pressured women to have sex and wondered why they resisted. The answer is simple: Nobody likes being used. Women want men to care about their happiness, which is impossible if a man is pushing a woman to give him something she doesn't want to give. (I recognize that in some relationships it can be the other way around, with the woman acting as the aggressor, but since it's usually the man exerting sexual pressure, I'm using that more common configuration. If your relationship doesn't fit the stereotype, simply reverse the sexes in the examples I provide.) But when men and women have a mutually loving, exclusive relationship, they almost always have a healthy desire to express their affection sexually. There is no aphrodisiac in the world equal to knowing that your partner genuinely cares about your happiness.

> There is nothing that will make you more sexually appealing to your partner than if he or she knows you genuinely care about his or her happiness.

When I gave the example of Bruce and Paula, I didn't mean to suggest that when there's a difference in sexual interest between two partners, the more "interested" (or more aggressive) partner should always do the learning or changing. Sometimes the more passive partner also has something important to learn, as was the case with Erica, who talked to me about her husband, Matt.

"Matt is always pushing me to have sex with him, and I hate it."

"So, earlier in your marriage, did you have sex more often than you do now?" I asked.

"Yes, we used to have a sex a lot, but I just don't enjoy it like I used to."

After we'd talked for a few minutes, the problem became clear. Like most couples, Matt and Erica fell in love because they found in each other a source of Imitation Love—praise, power, pleasure, safety—that they hoped would make them happy in the absence of Real Love. They got married because they hoped that source of "happiness" would last for a lifetime.

Without realizing it, Matt and Erica were obtaining their supply of Imitation Love by *trading* it with each other. In this case, we'll talk specifically about how they traded Imitation Love through sex. Each time they had sex early in their marriage, Matt received more physical pleasure than Erica enjoyed. Why then did she agree to this apparently unfair trade? Because she got just as much from sex as Matt did—but in *different forms* of Imitation Love. When they had sex, Erica felt desirable, worthwhile, and important—a combination of praise and power. In other words, it was still a good trade.

Over a period of years, however, Matt became far less flattering about Erica's sexual desirability than he had been, so that by the time Erica spoke to me, she felt much less important and more used than she had in the beginning of her marriage. Although Erica was still getting the same amount of physical pleasure from sex, she was receiving much less praise and power from the trade than she had in the beginning of their relationship. Matt, however, was getting the same amount of pleasure—greater than Erica was getting. In other words, the trade had become unbalanced. It was no wonder that Erica no longer wanted to participate.

I explained to Erica what Real Love is. I showed her how the absence of it had led to her unhappiness, and I told her what she could do to find it. In the meantime, I suggested something that could improve her sexual interactions with Matt.

"Your problem isn't with *sex,*" I said. "The problem is that you're using sex as *a form of Imitation Love,* and you don't think the trading is fair. Your problem will be solved when you stop using sex as a form of *Imitation Love* and start seeing it as an expression of *Real Love.*"

Erica looked puzzled. "What do you mean, *I'm* using sex as a form of Imitation Love? What about my husband?"

"Of course, you're right. He's doing the same thing, but we're not here to fix him. You can only work on yourself."

I explained again how *she* had been getting Imitation Love from sex in the form of praise, power, and pleasure, and how she could use this opportunity to eliminate Imitation Love from her relationship and replace it with Real Love.

"The important question," I said, "is this: Do you want your relationship to stay like it is, or do you want it to change?"

"I really want it to be different."

"Then don't keep waiting for your husband to approach *you* about sex. That just makes you feel more like a victim—you feel attacked and defensive. And stop looking at sex as something you trade with your husband. Or as something being done *to* you. You have an opportunity here to make a conscious decision to increase the unconditional love in your own life and in your relationship with Matt. You committed yourself to learn to love this man for a lifetime. Now you can choose to be more loving and change your relationship. Don't wait for him to approach *you.* Go to *him* and *offer* to have sex. You're not 'giving in' here, or being used. You're making a conscious choice to *love* him—and it doesn't matter whether or not he understands what you're doing or returns the love you're giving. If you can see sex as an expression of love and a way to become more loving yourself, the way you feel about it will change completely."

Erica paused. "But he doesn't care about me when we have sex."

"I understand that—and for a while he probably *will* continue to use you when you have sex—but someone in your relationship has to be willing to start the process of loving the other unconditionally, or it will never happen. Do you see that?"

She paused again. "I didn't think of that."

"You can do this. It isn't about sex. It's about learning how to share your love with your husband. You'll be offering him something he enjoys because you care about him, just like you'd cook him a favorite meal. Now, that *will be* easier to do if you feel more loved yourself. Remember what I told you about learning to tell the truth about yourself and finding Real Love? You've been doing that here with me. In our conversation, you've talked about yourself quite a lot. Have you felt accepted?"

"Until you asked," she said, "I hadn't thought about it, but, yes, I do feel accepted, and I've enjoyed it very much. I haven't had that feeling very often."

"At this moment, do you feel less angry at Matt than when you first started talking to me?"

She laughed. "Right now I don't feel angry at him at all."

"That's because when people feel loved, they lose their need to protect themselves with anger. The more you do this—talk to people who can see you and accept you—the easier it will be for you to be loving toward Matt."

Making sex a more fulfilling experience is rarely a question of making it more physically exciting. It's usually a question of learning to be more unconditionally loving. When we do that, the physical fulfillment follows naturally.

When Erica began to initiate sex with her husband, she found that giving her love freely, as a gift, made the sex far more enjoyable for her, both emotionally and physically. Of course, Matt was also delighted, and he asked Erica what had caused her change in attitude. Erica told him what she'd learned about Real Love and about her decision to offer him sex as a gift. After that conversation, Matt came to talk to me himself.

"We're having the best sex we've ever had in our lives," he said. "I'm enjoying it more than I ever have, and I've never seen *her* have this much fun. It's pretty amazing, actually. I don't want to do anything to ruin this. So what do I do if *I* want to have sex now? Do I have to wait until *she* wants to? I know that in the past I've pushed her to have sex, and that's made it unpleasant for her and hurt our relationship. So how do I handle it if *I* want sex?"

I discussed with Matt how to make a clear and loving request, as we discussed in Chapter Seven. We can request anything of our spouse—including sex—but when we expect or demand it, the results will not be compatible with a loving relationship. A real gift—like sex or Real Love—must be freely offered and freely received. In order to enrich the love in their relationship, Erica needed to offer herself freely to her husband, while Matt needed to do nothing that would pressure her to have sex with him (although he could make a request without expectations). It would have been very unproductive for him to remind her that she *should* be initiating sex with him. And he needed to be willing to hear *no* in response to his requests. They each had their own lessons to learn about how to have a mutually loving relationship.

———

Sex has become an awful experience for many of us. We worry about the adequacy of our sexual performance. We're afraid that our partner won't find us sexually desirable. And many of us live with the constant anxiety that our partner will touch us sexually, because we can't stand the thought of being used again by someone who doesn't really love us. Emptiness and fear utterly destroy the pleasure of sex, and impotence is often caused by fear. But when people feel unconditionally loved, most sexual dysfunction disappears.

If we really want to eliminate the unhappiness caused by the misuse of sex in the world, we need to teach our children about Real Love. Even better, we need to love them unconditionally, because what we learn in childhood we tend to carry throughout the rest of our lives. Our children need to understand that sex is a natural expression of affection to be shared between two people who have made a lifelong exclusive commitment to one another. They need to be involved in open discussions about sex that include guidance about dating, relationships, masturbation, pornography, how to have a conversation about feelings, and so on. Otherwise, we'll be exposing them to the song of the Sirens and the rocks on the shore.

The Truth About Parenting

Good parenting is not a technique, nor is it an opportunity to manipulate our children to behave in a way that's convenient for *us*. Good parenting is the natural result of remembering and providing those things children need most to be happy. More than anything else, our children need Real Love, and we therefore become better parents only as we learn to be more loving, not as we learn to make our children do what we want.

Families exist to provide a place where a child can feel unconditionally loved and can learn to love others. Of course, children also need to learn the four R's—reading, 'riting, 'rithmetic, and responsibility (the skills and attitudes that allow them to "survive in the real world")—but no matter how well they learn those things, if they don't learn how to love other people, they will not be happy.

> Good parenting is not a technique but a natural result of unconditionally loving and teaching our children.

When we don't feel loved, we tend to seek Imitation Love from the people around us, including our children. Unconsciously, we get "love" from our children in the form of respect, obedience, and gratitude. Certainly these *are* commendable qualities in a child, but a significant part of our motivation for insisting on these virtues is that they make *our* lives more convenient and allow us to feel more powerful and worthwhile as parents. We hate to admit to that selfishness, but we prove it every time we become disappointed and angry when our children fail to demonstrate these qualities. To put it bluntly, we often don't teach our children to be respectful, obedient, and grateful solely for *their* benefit. We do it because it fills *our* emptiness and soothes *our* fears in the absence of Real Love.

Our demands for our children's Imitation Love can seem quite innocent, but the effect is still devastating. For example, when a mother says, "Give Mommy a kiss," she unwittingly makes her child responsible for loving her. And that's obvious to the child, because Mommy smiles when he kisses her and frowns when he resists. Clearly, he controls her happiness as he chooses whether or not to love her in the way she demands. A child cannot feel unconditionally loved and happy while carrying the burden of making his parents happy. That's an unbearably heavy responsibility.

No parent ever has the right to expect love from a child. It's the responsibility of parents to teach and love their children, not the other way around.

The most common mistake we make as parents is to have insufficient Real Love in our own lives, because without that we simply cannot give our children the love they need.

During a break at a parenting seminar I was leading, a mother approached me with obvious agitation and asked, "How do I get my son to stop being angry and rebellious all the time?"

"Maybe you need to find out *why* he's angry before you try to *control* his anger," I suggested. "If a fire alarm goes off in a building, is it wise to simply turn it off, or should someone try to find out what triggered the alarm?"

"I never thought of it that way."

"You need to. Although he doesn't realize it himself, your son is telling you something with his anger and rebellion. His anger is a *reaction* to emptiness and fear. What he wants more than anything else is to feel unconditionally loved, and he doesn't feel that. His anger protects him—he feels less helpless and afraid when he's angry. I don't say this to blame you—like most parents, you've done your best with your son. You didn't know *how* to love him unconditionally, but that's something you can learn to do. When you feel loved enough yourself, you'll be able to give him what he needs—and then there's a strong possibility he'll stop being angry and rebellious."

"So you're saying that *I'm* the problem here?"

"Of course," I said gently. "As parents, we don't like hearing that very much, but it's obvious when we calm down and think about it. The one thing we all need most to be happy is Real Love. When we don't have that, we react with Getting and Protecting Behaviors, like anger. And who is most responsible for giving a child the Real Love he needs? His parents. In the case of your son, that would be you. You don't need to feel guilty about it, just motivated to get the Real Love you need to share with him."

Like that mother, we all want a quick fix for our children, but there isn't one. We must accept the fact that *we* are the primary problem in our children's lives. How could it be otherwise? Who taught our children their values, their fears, and their Getting and Protecting Behaviors? *We* did, but then we want to place the blame for our children's problems on *them,* their peers, the schools, television—anywhere but on ourselves. That's nonsense.

> When our children are angry, rebellious, or otherwise difficult, they're reacting to insufficient Real Love in their lives, and we parents always have a major responsibility for that.

Fortunately, we are more than our children's primary *problem.* We're also their greatest *opportunity* for happiness. Children who do feel unconditionally loved by their parents are the happiest creatures on the planet. They simply don't have a *need* to drink, smoke, yell at their parents, fight with their siblings, act out in school, use extreme forms of entertainment, and have indiscriminate sex. We can see the proof of that again and again as we learn to tell the truth about ourselves, feel loved, and learn to give our children the Real Love they require to be happy.

Whenever I speak about loving our children unconditionally, at least one person is sure to protest, "But somebody has to discipline them. If we don't do that as parents, how will they ever learn?" Loving our children unconditionally does not mean we say and do nothing when they make mistakes. Children do need to be corrected, but they do not need the disappointment and anger we almost always administer along with the instruction we offer. The moment we're irritated, our children correctly sense that we don't love them unconditionally, and the effect is always disastrous.

Although we're mostly unaware of it, we use our disappointment and anger to control our children's behavior. They will often do what we want in order to avoid our expression of those terrible feelings, but that eliminates the possibility of their feeling unconditional love from us. Being permissive with children, however, is as destructive as controlling them. What children need—and what most of us have never seen—is correction that is given with genuine acceptance. That's Real Love.

There is no job in the world more important than being a parent, but our behavior testifies that we don't believe that. Instead of devoting ourselves to learning how to teach and unconditionally love our children, we tend to invest our time and effort in careers, money, entertainment, and impressing other people. The harvest of that approach has been unhappy children whose behaviors are designed to get Imitation Love and to protect themselves. Only as we find Real Love for ourselves and share it with our children will that harvest change.

Family, Friends, Co-workers, and Everyone Else

The most worthwhile goal of any relationship is to receive and give Real Love. We can practice telling the truth, feeling loved, and loving other people as we associate with family, friends, co-workers, and even total strangers.

Siblings

Siblings have many opportunities to learn about Real Love as they interact with each other, especially when they're assisted by loving parents.

Some time ago, I overheard two of my children, Benjamin and Janette, talking in the next room. "You're wearing my shirt again!" shouted Benjamin.

"You wear my clothes, too! You have no right to talk!" Janette responded with considerable irritation.

"But you never put anything back," Benjamin went right on. "I'll never see that shirt again. I don't want you touching my stuff!"

Parents often step in at this point to resolve the dispute. When they do that, they create peace for themselves, but they rob their children of valuable opportunities to learn about seeing and loving each other.

I could easily have made this conflict go away *for me* by telling my children to stop arguing, or by telling Janette not to touch Benjamin's stuff again, which is the approach I'd used for years. But there was a more important lesson to be learned. I went into the room where they were arguing and spoke to Benjamin. "You look angry," I said.

"Sure I am," he said. "She's wearing my shirt again, and I'm sick of it."

"So it's *her* fault you're angry?"

"Yes," he agreed.

"If I gave you twenty million dollars in cash right now, and a new car of your choice, would you still be angry at Janette?"

Benjamin smiled. "Probably not."

"Then it couldn't be *her* fault that you're angry, could it?"

I then told Benjamin the story we discussed in Chapter Five about the two dollars on the table and the twenty million in the bank (pp. 117–118). I explained that he was angry only because he felt like he was down to his last two dollars in the world—he was unloved and empty—and in that condition virtually anything anyone did would have made him feel more empty and threatened. His anger was just a way to protect himself.

"The reason you're down to your last two dollars—the reason you feel unloved and empty—is *my fault*. It has nothing to do with Janette. You don't feel unconditionally loved because, in the past, I told you in many ways that I didn't love you when you made mistakes and when you didn't do what I wanted—mostly by getting angry at you. We've talked about that before."

Benjamin nodded his understanding, so I continued. "When Janette took something of yours without asking, you felt like one more person was telling you she didn't care about you. You were already overly sensitive because of the times *I'd* been unloving toward you. But none of this is Janette's fault, even though it's true that she was *not* being thoughtful of you when she wore your shirt without asking you. You hate feeling unloved, and to protect yourself from that feeling you got angry. People feel less helpless and afraid when they get angry—they feel strong and tough. But as I love you more, and as you feel more loved, you'll feel like you have twenty million dollars all the time, and you'll have much less need to protect yourself by getting angry."

Janette got angry at Benjamin for the same reason Benjamin got angry at her—she didn't feel loved. When Benjamin

> Parents need to view arguments between children not as inconveniences to be stopped, but as opportunities to teach them about Real Love.

confronted her, she felt threatened and defended herself with the Protecting Behavior that was most familiar to her.

When both children understood the cause of their anger, and felt loved by me while they were being truthful about their selfishness, their anger disappeared. In time, as they felt more loved by me and had additional opportunities to see and love each other, their relationship became far more loving.

Friends

Our friends give us wonderful opportunities to make choices and learn how to love each other unconditionally.

Lewis and Ray lived an hour apart, and for years they'd been meeting every Wednesday for dinner. Because Ray didn't like to drive, they usually picked a spot closer to his house. But Lewis didn't really like the fact that he had to do most of the driving, and he complained about it to a wise friend. "It's not fair," said Lewis. "We always do whatever's convenient for Ray, and I'm tired of doing all the driving."

The wise man smiled. "A relationship is the natural result of people making independent choices. This relationship will work only if you allow Ray to make his own choice; then you can make yours."

"But I do all the driving," said Lewis, "and I think—"

The wise man interrupted. "You're describing what you *want*. Ray has chosen to drive less than you do, and he gets to make that choice. Now, what do *you* choose to do?"

"But it's not fair—"

"Irrelevant," the wise man interrupted again. "You can only make *your own* choice. So far, you've chosen to do most of the driving. But you've also *chosen* to resent Ray and try to change him, and *that's* what's making you unhappy, not what Ray is doing."

The wise man then explained the Law of Choice, which

we discussed in Chapter Three, and offered Lewis the other choices that were available to him:

1. He could stop trying to change Ray but still resent him for the unequal travel arrangements. His relationship with Ray would then be strained and unhappy (live with it and hate it).
2. He could continue traveling and simply enjoy the time he got to spend with his friend (live with it and like it). That choice would only be possible, however, after Lewis learned to tell the truth about himself and to feel unconditionally loved. Without feeling more Real Love in his life, he wouldn't be likely to really *enjoy* an "unfair" relationship with Ray—he would only *tolerate it*.
3. He could choose to drive less himself and meet with Ray less often. This choice would give them less time together, but Lewis would be less inconvenienced and resentful (a variation on living with it and liking it).
4. He could choose to end his relationship with Ray (leave it). This would almost certainly be a happier choice for Lewis than trying to change Ray, and better than the frustration and resentment created by his failure to change him.

Lewis's friend also explained what he'd learned about Real Love and how to find it. After that, Lewis chose to tell the truth about himself to people who could love him. As he felt more loved, he began to see Ray clearly and to accept him as he was instead of expecting him to change. As he felt more loving toward Ray, he decided he was willing to keep doing most of the driving, and he also saw that his selfishness had ruined relationships with many other people over the years.

When we try to change other people, we're really choosing

to be miserable. Most of us prove that every day, but we still continue to do it.

Strangers

Even as we interact with complete strangers, we can learn about feeling loved, making choices, and accepting other people.

Bill often became angry at other drivers when he was on his way home in heavy traffic. He talked to a wise friend about one such experience with traffic. "I learned something on my way home from work today," said Bill. "Some guy cut in front of me, and I had to slam on my brakes to keep from hitting him."

"What did you do?" asked his friend.

"I was furious that this fool could be so thoughtless," Bill said, "and I was about to honk the horn and scream at him when I remembered that every time I'm angry, it's not some-body else's fault. I've learned that my anger is always a reaction to *my* feeling empty and afraid. As I thought about that, I remembered that quite a few people—like you, for in-stance—really do love me. And I realized that some stupid driver cutting me off couldn't change that. I still didn't like what he did—it startled me and inconvenienced me—but I wasn't angry at him."

"Felt good, didn't it?"

"Amazing. I really do have a choice. When I remember that I'm loved, I don't feel angry at anyone. I like having a choice instead of always getting angry and feeling miserable."

We can all learn to see and love people everywhere, even people we interact with only once. Rather than seeing the people around us as an inconvenience when they don't give us what we want, we can learn to see them as an opportunity to be accepting.

> ◯ Even with complete strangers we have opportunities to practice unconditional acceptance.

Real Love in the Workplace

In the world of profit and loss, it may seem strange to talk about Real Love. However, in the workplace we're always dealing with *people,* and those people can never be separated from their need for unconditional love.

As I said in Chapter Three, a promise is "an agreement on the part of one person to perform a specific act." If two people exchange promises, they have a contract. A contract is not a relationship. Whereas expectations are destructive in a loving relationship, clear and mutual expectations *are* an accepted part of any contract. For example, as employees we have a contract with our employer that gives us the right to expect him to pay us in exchange for our doing the job we were hired to perform. However, we have *no* right to expect our employer to give us anything that's not specified in the contract, such as compassion or praise, which are elements of a relationship, not a contract. Larry had these inappropriate expectations at his job.

He worked hard to impress his boss. He advertised his successes and always looked busy and cheerful when the boss was around. For his efforts, however, he expected more than a paycheck; he also expected approval and praise. That was a natural but inappropriate desire that resulted from Larry's not feeling unconditionally loved all his life. Unfortunately, Larry's effort to earn Imitation Love had two negative effects: First, it exhausted him and distracted him from performing well at his job. Second, his boss sensed that he was being manipulated for approval and tended to avoid Larry, thereby withdrawing the praise Larry was seeking in the first place.

Without realizing it, most of us expect our employers to "love" us in some way. We prove we have those expectations each time we complain that we're not appreciated or respected, which means we're not getting enough Imitation Love in the absence of Real Love. Similarly, most employers inappropriately expect some kind of Imitation Love (praise, power, safety) from their employees, in addition to the contractual agreement to do the job they were hired for.

Even in business, however, having a contract with someone doesn't prevent us from also having a good relationship with that same person.

Harold had the same boss as Larry, but Harold knew he was loved and worthwhile, because he'd been telling the truth about himself for a long time to his wife and several friends who had accepted him unconditionally. Because of that, he didn't have the need to manipulate the boss to "love" him and make him feel good. The boss felt that absence of manipulation from Harold and therefore enjoyed being around him. Because of that, they had a positive *relationship* in addition to their business contract. When we've received enough Real Love, the effect on all our relationships—even those at work—is profound.

The boss came to work one day in a terrible mood. He snapped at Larry and Harold about something that wasn't going well on the job.

Because Larry needed the boss to make him feel worthwhile, he felt attacked and hurt. He then protected himself from the feeling of being alone and helpless by acting like a victim. He criticized the boss behind his back and denied his part of the responsibility for the problem the boss was complaining about.

Harold, however, already felt loved and worthwhile, so he didn't feel threatened. Rather, he was able to see the situation clearly and help solve the problem. Harold knew the boss was afraid he'd look bad because of the mistakes that were being made on the job, and that the boss's anger was both an unconscious effort to protect himself from feeling helpless and an attempt to intimidate other people into doing what he wanted. Of course, the boss felt accused and attacked by Larry, but seen and accepted by Harold.

In every relationship, even at work, we can learn to see and accept our partners, as Harold did. That's Real Love.

> All the conflicts we have with people at work can be understood once we see the lack of Real Love and the Getting and Protecting Behaviors of everyone involved, including ourselves.

I suggest that most problems in the workplace do not result from a lack of information, insufficient technology, or poor management techniques but from a lack of Real Love. Notice what happened when the boss was angry at Larry. Larry reacted by lying, attacking, acting like a victim, and running. These behaviors entirely paralyzed his potential productivity, and the same thing happens every day with people and entire departments in corporations everywhere.

Imagine how positively productivity would be affected if people felt unconditionally loved and were able to apply all their energy to the goals of the company rather than being continually distracted by acquiring praise, power, and pleasure, or the need to protect themselves. Imagine how positively corporate leadership would be affected if executives felt unconditionally loved and loving, and were motivated by a desire to enhance the happiness and productivity of their employees rather than by the desire to protect *themselves* and build up their own kingdoms of praise, power, and safety. Real Love matters very much in the world of business.

Our Relationship with God

Imagine communicating by e-mail with a creature who lives on a planet where there is no water. How would you describe an ocean to him? It's very difficult for anyone to imagine something when he or she has never experienced anything remotely like it. But if you brought one of those aliens to Earth and sat him beside a stream, he would soon understand a great deal about water, and it's very likely that he would understand your description of an ocean.

Similarly, most of us have never seen consistent unconditional love, and that is why we have a confusing relationship—or none at all—with God, whose most important characteristic is perfect love. When we begin to feel the unconditional love of wise men and women, it's like seeing our first drop of water. Knowing that water exists, we can begin to imagine a God who offers us an ocean of love. I have been impressed with the consistency of this process. Most people who learn to tell the truth about themselves and find the unconditional love of other people eventually develop a more loving relationship with God.

> As we feel the Real Love of other human beings, we naturally strengthen our connection to God, the source of perfect and infinite love.

Our ability to love each other is often severely affected by our emptiness and fear. But God isn't affected by those feelings and can therefore love us perfectly. When we exercise faith, we can learn to feel the abundance of God's perfect love and, therefore, never feel afraid or alone. In the absence of emptiness and fear, seeing and loving other people become natural and effortless. Therefore, a loving relationship with God is the greatest gift in this life, and it is equally available to all of us.

Dealing with Obstacles on the Path to Real Love

Disappointment, Anger, and Getting
and Protecting Behaviors

After teaching my son Benjamin to drive, I took him to the motor vehicle bureau for the driving portion of his test. In our state, the driving exam is conducted on a closed course with simulated railroad crossings, parking situations, and so on. Although he had driven quite well during the year I was teaching him, Benjamin was still nervous about passing his test and finally getting his driver's license, and his anxiety affected his judgment during the exam. At one point, he made a right turn, and becoming confused about the lane markings on the new road, he drove in the lane reserved for oncoming traffic. Later, when he was asked to demonstrate his parallel parking ability, he knocked over one of the orange cones representing a parked car. As a result, he failed the test, and when he informed me of the outcome, he said, "But I only knocked over one cone, and I was only in the wrong lane for a little while before I got back in the right one. I did all the rest of the test right." I explained to him that while I still considered him a good driver, the test results were nevertheless fair. If the cone had been a car, and if the oncoming lane had been filled with traffic, the consequences would have been significantly worse than a failed exam. Sometimes it doesn't matter how many times we do some things right. If we hit certain obstacles, the consequences of those mistakes can instantly wipe out the effects of all our positive efforts.

Similarly, even though we tell the truth about ourselves, find Real Love, and share it with others, we can quickly lose the effect of those positive experiences if we hit certain obstacles in our lives. We must, therefore, learn to identify those obstacles and deal with them effectively, or they can destroy our happiness.

Eliminating Conflict

When I talk about conflict, I don't mean simple disagreement. Rather, I mean any interaction that involves disappointment or anger. It's possible to disagree without becoming involved in a conflict, and it's the conflict, not the disagreement, that harms relationships.

As we all practice making our own choices, we unavoidably disagree about the way many things should be done, and when that happens, we often inconvenience and injure one another. These moments of disagreement can then lead to enormous disappointment and anger, and a single such experience can sometimes destroy the effects of many loving moments. Think about how you feel when someone becomes angry at you, even after you've had many positive interactions with that same person. A single hateful argument can neutralize the effect of a hundred words of acceptance. Experts often propose ways to "manage" these conflicts, but I suggest that we not settle for the superficial and temporary effect of such techniques and learn instead to *eliminate* as much conflict as

possible by filling our lives with unconditional love and genuine happiness.

––––

In order to eliminate the terrible effects of conflict from our
lives, we must understand and live according to two important principles. First, Real Love. When we feel unconditionally loved, we have the one thing that's key to our happiness.
In the presence of Real Love, emptiness, fear, and anger evap-
orate, and those are the essential elements of every conflict. In
short, Real Love eliminates conflict altogether, rather than
managing or suppressing it.

Second, the Law of Choice. We can all *expect* to be loved
and happy. However, we do *not* have the right to expect any
single person or group of people to love us or make us happy.
When we do that, we place our own needs above theirs and
deny the Law of Choice, which, as we explained in Chapter
Three, states that "everyone has the right to choose what he
or she says and does." When we truly believe that other people have the right to make their own choices, we don't feel
disappointed in them, nor do we get angry when they make a
choice with which we disagree. Without anger and disappointment, there's nothing to fuel a conflict, and it will die
from a lack of energy.

> ✐ We eliminate conflict when we genuinely care
> about the happiness of our partners and allow them to
> make their own choices.

We create conflict, on the other hand, when we demand
that other people respond to us in any particular way. When
we do that, we deny their freedom to choose, and what we get
won't feel like Real Love. William's mother guaranteed her

own unhappiness when she failed to freely allow her son to make his own choices.

Each year, William traveled to visit his parents during the Christmas holiday. One year he decided to stay home, and his mother was not happy with the news. "But you promised!" she complained. "And I've really been counting on your visit."

Throughout their brief conversation, she acted disappointed and offended. But William had a right to make his own choice about where to spend his time. He was not *responsible* for making his mother happy, which does not mean that he didn't *care* about her happiness.

We can have a genuine concern for another person's well-being without giving that person everything he or she wants. We are not required to prove our love to everyone in the ways they demand. If we did that, there would be no end to the proving, and the Law of Choice would go out the window. Rather, while I am learning to unconditionally love you, I must make my own choices about how to contribute to your happiness from moment to moment—if indeed I choose to contribute at all. You can't make those choices for me. If you controlled me in any way, you couldn't feel that I was offering you anything of my own choice, and you wouldn't feel loved.

Because William's mother didn't feel unconditionally loved, she constantly manipulated other people to get attention and praise, and to make herself feel important. When her manipulations failed to get her the Imitation Love she was seeking from William in the form of a visit, she experienced the miserable and desperate condition of having neither Real Love nor Imitation Love. That is an intolerable feeling, and it's only natural that she would then express disappointment and pain. When we're already empty and afraid, every failure to get the Imitation Love we seek becomes a major disappointment.

William, however, did not "make" his mother unhappy.

He simply gave her an opportunity to feel how empty her life had been for a very long time. Every time we're angry—and often when we're disappointed—we declare our expectation that someone else should abandon his or her own choices and give us what we want. When we do that—as William's mother did—we negatively affect our relationship with that person and further destroy our own happiness.

Carl and Laurie further illustrate why it is so important for us to follow the Law of Choice if we want to eliminate conflicts. After years of marriage, this couple had grown tired of their constant arguments, so they each found wise men and women who could help them tell the truth about themselves and feel loved. But as they learned to be loving with each other, they still naturally had occasional disagreements that turned into conflicts.

On one such occasion, Laurie was tired and didn't want to prepare the evening meal, so she asked Carl to go out with her to a restaurant. But Carl was also tired and said he preferred to stay home. Instead of having their usual argument, they remembered the Fourth Rule of Seeing, and Laurie called a wise friend for advice.

"This is easy," said the wise man. "You can both have what you want. Laurie, you can go out and Carl can stay home."

"But I want Carl to go with me," Laurie protested.

"You don't get to choose what Carl does, only what *you* do. You've indicated that you want three things: first, to eat a meal you don't have to prepare; second, to get out of the house for a while; and third, to spend some time with Carl. You can do all that if you go out, eat by yourself, and then return home to spend the rest of the evening with Carl. Or you could go out and get a meal to bring back and eat with Carl. No problem."

"But I want to go out to dinner *with* Carl."

"And I'd love to have an extra thousand dollars right now, but does that give me the right to steal it from *you*?"

"Of course not," she said.

"That's what you're doing with Carl. You believe that if you want something, *he's* obligated to give it to you. That belief will destroy your relationship. We only have the right to make choices about *our own* behavior. We can't control other people's choices to get what we want."

Requests and Expectations

In the above situation, Laurie no doubt thought she was making a "request" of Carl, but when she became disappointed and somewhat annoyed at his response, it was obvious to her wise friend that her "request" was really a demand, which means that she *expected* Carl to respond in a particular way—the way she wanted him to. Sometimes our expectations are disguised by the fact that we're simply getting everything we want. Under those conditions, our disappointment and anger are hidden and reveal themselves only when we don't get what we "request." Eventually, however, with enough love and practice, we will be able to make appropriate and loving requests instead of demands.

As I've said many times, it's not appropriate to expect people to do things *for* us, but we *can* always expect them to stop doing things *to* us. For example, I don't have the right to expect you to love me, but I *can* insist that you stop hitting me. Even if you ignore my request to stop hitting me, however, I'm never justified in being angry. Anger is always selfish and makes happiness impossible. But if you choose to keep hitting me, I'd be foolish to live with it and like it or live with it and hate it, two of the choices we described in Chapter

Three. Rather, I would choose to leave the situation, and if necessary I'd physically defend myself until I could leave safely. When you feel sufficiently loved, it *is* possible to protect yourself without being angry.

Even when we think we're asking someone to stop doing something *to* us, however, we need to be sure we understand what's really going on. Sometimes, we're so used to our Getting and Protecting Behaviors that we might *think* a person is doing something *to* us when in fact we're really the one responsible for our own unhappiness.

Carl, for example, had learned as a child to withdraw (running) from threatening experiences, while Laurie had learned to protect herself by attacking. And so, as adults, they naturally continued to use those same Protecting Behaviors.

What Carl feared most was being criticized, and when he sensed Laurie's disapproval, he simply quit talking, or left the room, or spent more time at work—all forms of running. Laurie's greatest fear was feeling unloved and alone, which is what she always experienced when Carl withdrew from her. To protect herself, she criticized him and made him feel guilty for not spending more time with her as a "good husband" should.

Laurie demanded that Carl stop withdrawing from her, and Carl complained that Laurie always criticized him. They were locked in a terribly destructive cycle of protecting themselves by using the very behaviors that frightened their partner the most. Finally, they shared their problem with a wise friend who explained that they both had been violating the Law of Choice.

"Laurie," said the wise man, "Carl gets to make his own choices. You don't have the right to demand that he do what you want."

"But I do have the right to insist that he stop doing something *to* me, right?"

"Yes."

"When he withdraws, that hurts me, so he *is* doing something *to* me. And I have the right to tell him to stop it."

The wise man grinned. "No, you don't. Using that reasoning, you could force everyone to do whatever you wanted just by saying you'd be hurt if they didn't give you what you demanded. You could control the whole world with that reasoning. Do you see that?"

"But he *does* hurt me when he withdraws. How do I get him to stop it?"

"You don't," said the wise man, as he began to explain how unproductive it is to ever control our partners. "And in any case," he continued, "*Carl* isn't really hurting you. What you feel is empty and unloved, and that's been going on since long before you met Carl. Now you expect him to love you and make up for all the pain from your past. When he doesn't do that, you blame him for the pain you've felt all your life."

"So where do I get loved? Isn't that what husbands are for?"

"That would be nice—and eventually Carl might be able to love you in the way you need—but *right now* it's obvious that *neither* of you is capable of loving anyone unconditionally."

The wise man then explained how Laurie could find people capable of loving her unconditionally and take that Real Love back to share with her husband.

Resolving Differences or Disagreements

Even as Carl and Laurie learned how to tell the truth about themselves to loving men and women, and to love one another, they were still different people, and inevitably they still had different preferences about many things. That's unavoidable. But when they felt loved, those *differences* didn't have to result in *conflict*.

There came a time when Laurie again said to Carl, "I don't

really want to prepare a meal tonight. Can we go out and get something to eat?" This time, however, the results were very different.

"I'd love to spend some time with you," Carl replied, "but I'm really too tired to get out of this chair."

"Then maybe I could go out and get something to bring back for both of us. Is that all right with you?"

"Perfect. Thanks for doing that."

No matter how loving we become, we'll always have some *differences* or *disagreements* with our partner about everyday things—scheduling, money, meals, movies, whatever. But as long as we can readily and consistently handle these differences lovingly, they will not become *conflicts,* which always involve disappointment and anger. Differences remain insignificant if we remember the following principles:

- Find Real Love
- Make clear requests
- Accept your partner's decision

> In any relationship, there will always be simple differences or disagreements, but Real Love eliminates the disappointment and anger that turn disagreements into conflicts.

When people love each other, they don't try to get their way at the expense of their partner. They share information and make requests until both of them are satisfied with the result. And each partner then accepts the decision made by the other. In mutually loving relationships, you don't solve differences by winning an argument, giving in, or even compromising. You don't have to give your partner everything he or she asks for, and you won't get everything you want, either.

You just do your best to care about each other's happiness as you make decisions.

Controlling other people is selfish and wrong. We're never justified in demanding that our partners do what we want—not when we badly need it, not when they have more than enough to give, and not even when they're married to us.

Eliminating Conflict by Taking the Five Steps to Eliminating Our Own Disappointment and Anger

As I suggested at the beginning of this chapter, it's not disagreement that causes unhappiness—it's disappointment and anger. If we can learn to eliminate those feelings in ourselves, not only will we be happier, but also we can virtually eliminate conflict in our relationships, since our partners will find it difficult to stay in conflict with us when we're loving and happy. In the discussion that follows I'm going to be talking primarily about eliminating anger, since disappointment usually differs from anger only in degree.

Every time you find yourself becoming irritated or unhappy, take one or more of the following steps. They can be taken in any order and repeated many times.

- Be quiet
- Be wrong
- Feel loved
- Get loved
- Be loving

Be Quiet. Why would you ever knowingly destroy your own happiness or the love you want in your relationship? But that's what you do every time you speak to your partner in anger. If your car stalled in the middle of the highway, would you try to start it again by pouring gasoline on it and setting it on fire? That's just how absurd it is every time we speak to our partners in anger. When you're angry, you will not say anything loving or productive, and therefore, when you're angry, *do not speak*. Sharon and I had a conversation about this principle.

Sharon always had a great excuse for speaking to her husband when she was angry. It usually began with the words "But he . . ."

"When was the last time you spoke to him in anger and ended your conversation feeling genuinely happy and loving?" I asked her. "Or the two of you felt closer to each other?"

Obviously, she couldn't think of such a time, and she agreed to try not speaking when she was angry. But she had a question: "What can I do if I decide to be quiet and *he* keeps arguing? I can't just sit there with my mouth shut and look stupid, can I?"

"You can always say this," I told her. "Just say, '*I* am just not feeling loving enough to continue this conversation. We need to finish this later.' Notice that when you say that, you're not blaming your husband. *You're* taking all the responsibility for being wrong and stopping the conversation."

A few days later Sharon called me and said, "I told my husband exactly what you said. I said, 'I'm not feeling loving enough to continue this conversation,' and he just kept yelling at me. What am I supposed to do when he does that?"

"You still have lots of options, but I suggest two to start. You could say nothing at all and wait for him to run out of steam—which he will usually do if you don't add anger to the conflict—or you could just repeat what you said."

"I repeated it twice, but he kept yelling at me, and I got tired of it."

"You could go into another room."

"I did that, too."

"Go outside," I said.

238 • *Real Love*

"You're kidding."

"Do you want to stop the conflict in your relationship or not? It's not likely he'll keep yelling at you in front of the whole neighborhood."

"Actually, he might."

"Then get in the car and drive away."

If you're serious about not wanting to participate in a conflict, you don't have to. Sharon did what I suggested, and her husband eventually understood that she would not fight with him anymore.

Does this mean you can never disagree with your partner? Of course not. You can always state your opinion, even firmly. You can make requests. You don't have to give your partner everything he or she wants. But any time you bring anger into an interaction, you're being foolish.

Be Wrong. I simply cannot keep up my end of a conflict when I admit that I'm wrong—can you? When you admit that you're wrong, the fire of the conflict will die for a lack of fuel. So, any time you feel disappointment or anger, repeat, *"If I'm disappointed or angry, I'm wrong,"* and you won't be able to maintain those feelings for long.

Of course, you need to be able to identify *how* you're wrong when you're angry. If you can't do that, simply saying you're wrong becomes a meaningless technique. Unfortunately, however, when you're angry, you've already focused on your *partner's* faults, so you may need some help seeing how *you* are wrong. Try to think about the following:

1. As you're interacting with your partner, which is more important: to be angry and insist on being right, or to feel loved and to be loving? You can't have both. You can't be angry and also hope to make a loving, positive contribu-

tion to your relationship. You have to choose one course. Which of those two decisions will lead to a loving relationship and to greater happiness in your life? Is there *any* doubt about that? And if being loving is the better decision, the *right* thing to do, what does that make anger every time? Anger is wrong and must be eliminated before you can address the disagreement itself.

When you're angry, you might actually be right about *something* in that interaction, but that fact becomes meaningless in light of the destruction you cause with your anger. Your puny "rightness" will never outweigh the loss of Real Love caused by your anger.

2. Anger is a Getting and Protecting Behavior. It's a reaction to emptiness and fear, two conditions that make us blind to the needs and fears of other people. *Anger is a sure sign to us that we cannot see our partner clearly.* When we're angry, we're blind—we are *wrong*. It is most unwise to continue speaking in that condition.

3. A relationship is, as we've discussed, a natural result of people making independent choices. If you're angry, you're trying to control your partner's choices, and you're ruining the possibility of a loving relationship. You're violating the Law of Choice and the Law of Expectations. Is that really what you want to do?

To summarize: When you're angry, you're unloving, blind, trying to control your partner, and expecting him or her to make you happy. You couldn't be any more wrong.

So, to whom do you say, "If I'm angry, I'm wrong"? If possible, say it to the person you're angry at, which will create the possibility both of eliminating the conflict and of being loved by your partner. Or, if your partner isn't capable of accepting you, say it to a wise man or woman, which will give you a chance to feel loved. Sometimes just saying it to yourself will be enough to make a big difference. In fact, on some occasions we have no one else to say it *to*—such as when we're angry because we're stuck in traffic.

> When you're angry, you're unloving, blind, trying to control your partner, and expecting him or her to make you happy. You couldn't be more wrong.

Feel Loved (Remember That You're Loved). We become afraid in a conflict—and subsequently react with anger—only when we don't feel loved. When we're absolutely certain that we're loved—when we have that one thing that matters most in all the world—the disagreements and anger of other people are no longer threatening to us. With Real Love, we don't become afraid and have no *need* to get angry.

In that sense, getting angry can actually be useful as a reminder that you need to make a conscious effort to remember the Real Love you've been given. If you can do that—if you can reach in and draw from the love that's already in your bucket—you will greatly reduce or even eliminate your emptiness and fear. Your anger will then have no function and will soon vanish.

Of course, you can only *remember* that you're loved if you've previously taken the steps to find Real Love and have actually felt the acceptance and love of wise men and women. Once you've done that, you can carry the memory with you everywhere you go. In the last chapter, when Bill got angry because he was cut off in heavy traffic (p. 221), he didn't have access to anyone who could love him. But he *remembered* that he was loved, and his anger disappeared.

Remembering that we're loved can also prevent anger from

starting, as it did for Mark, whom we met in Chapter Five (pp. 118–119). Mark had an opportunity to react to his wife with anger, but when he remembered the love of his friends, he hugged her instead of getting angry at her, and his unconditional love reduced her to tears. Real Love eliminated his fear and therefore his *need* to get angry. It can do the same for all of us.

Get Loved. Sometimes it's not enough simply to remember we've been loved. We need to feel loved in the present. Remember Janet from Chapter Four (pp. 101–2), who was so angry at her boss? When she got angry the *second time,* she did remember that she was loved by her wise friend, but that wasn't enough to eliminate her anger. To do that, she still needed to call her friend, tell the truth about herself, and feel her friend's acceptance and love.

Notice that Janet's anger—and her conflict with her boss—was not resolved by some clever technique of communication. It was resolved as Janet took all four of the steps we've discussed thus far. First, she exercised self-control and *kept quiet.* She then *remembered that she was loved* well enough to call her wise friend and tell the truth about herself—that she was unloving and afraid. And, as she did that, she took the step of *being wrong* by speaking a variation of the words "If I'm angry, I'm wrong," thereby telling the truth about herself and creating an opportunity to *feel unconditionally loved.*

Be Loving (Do Something Loving). Being filled with Real Love is certainly an advantage when you're attempting to love others. However, as I've already said, you don't have to wait until you're filled with love before you attempt to give it to other people. The miracle of Real Love is that it can often multiply as you give it. And for that reason, you can sometimes eliminate your anger simply by *choosing* to do something uncondition-ally loving. Jim discovered the truth of that as he loved his wife, Stephanie.

Because Jim worked full-time and Stephanie worked only part-time, she had agreed always to have the house clean and a meal prepared when Jim got home from work. But she often failed to fulfill her commitment, and that was a source of frequent conflict between them. One day when Jim got home from work, he found the kitchen a mess, and for the third time that week dinner was not ready.

Having learned the five steps to eliminate his anger, he was determined this time to do something different. He first made a decision to not speak to Stephanie while he was irri-tated. Then he repeated several times to himself that he was wrong to be angry—and he believed it. He remembered that there were people who loved him unconditionally, and he called a wise man, who listened to him and accepted him while he told the truth about the selfishness of his anger.

But even after all that, Jim was still irritated with Stephanie, so he decided to *do* something loving. He cleaned up the kitchen. He washed the dishes, put everything on the counters away, and actually started mopping the floor, some-thing he hadn't done since he was in the army. To his own amazement, the more things he did for her, the less selfish and angry he felt. When Stephanie got home, she couldn't be-lieve her eyes. Jim threw his arms around her and told her he loved her. What might have been a conflict became instead a powerfully loving experience for both of them.

I recognize that when you're angry, you may not *feel* like doing something loving. In that case, try taking the other steps first, as Jim did. There are many loving things you can do for people when you're angry at them, depending on the nature of your relationship.

1. Perform an act of service for him or her.
2. Look your partner in the eye and, instead of avoiding him or her, have a friendly conversation. That alone can be a very loving act.
3. Thank your partner—in person, on the phone, with a card of appreciation—for something he or she did for you.
4. Take him or her out for a quiet meal and conversation.
5. Touch your partner. It's difficult to stay angry at someone you're gently touching on the hand.
6. Tell him you love him. Tell her you love her.
7. You know your partners. You know what they'd like.
8. Perform an act of service for *someone else*. As you've learned by now, when you share the love you have, you somehow end up with more than you had when you started. Therefore, loving anyone at all can make you feel more loving toward the person you're angry at.

When we're angry, it's good to take the steps that are required to stop the flow of anger and *get love* for ourselves. However, we also need to make a conscious choice to actively *express our love* and experience the miracle that often accompanies that experience.

> When you're angry at your partner, you may not feel like doing something loving for him or her. But if you do it anyway, you'll create an opportunity for *both* of you to feel the miracle of Real Love in your lives.

If you'll remember to take these five steps when you get angry, you'll slowly eliminate conflict and, therefore, one of the biggest obstacles to Real Love and happiness in your life.

Dealing with Getting and Protecting Behaviors

Although lying, attacking, acting like a victim, and running destroy relationships and interfere with our own ability to feel loved, most of us still do one or more of these things every day. What can we do about that? What can we do when we find ourselves once again using the behaviors that can only make us unhappy? For one thing, we need simply to exercise some self-control and make a conscious decision to stop using them. But we also need to remember that Getting and Protecting Behaviors are only reactions to the absence of Real Love. Once we've done that, the solution is obvious: We need to tell the truth about ourselves and create the opportunity to feel unconditionally accepted. As we feel loved, we simply have no *need* for Getting and Protecting Behaviors.

And what happens when we encounter Getting and Protecting Behaviors in *other people*? How do we respond? Other people use these behaviors for the same reasons we do—because they feel empty and afraid in the absence of Real Love. We can reduce their emptiness and fear as we bring Real Love into our interactions. We do that as we tell the truth about ourselves and as we accept and love our partners. The worst thing we can do is protect ourselves or try to get other people to like us. That would only make them feel more empty and afraid, and then they'd be even more likely to use Getting and Protecting Behaviors.

In short, *telling the truth about ourselves is part of the solution* in all situations where Getting and Protecting Behaviors arise, whether in ourselves or in others. This approach creates opportunities for us to feel accepted and loved, and it's also very reassuring to other people when they're empty and afraid. As I discuss each of the Getting and Protecting Behaviors, I'll illustrate how this approach works.

When We Lie

Most of us lie every day, and we often don't know we're doing it, which makes it impossible to stop.

Andrew often ate lunch with his co-workers. They were all athletes and outdoorsmen, so they usually talked about things like sports and hunting. Andrew, however, had little experience with those activities, and so he rarely spoke. One day he mentioned to a wise friend that he felt uncomfortable with the other men at work.

"That's because you're lying to them," said the wise man.

"Lying?" said Andrew, surprised. "How?"

"When they talk about football, do you admit you don't know much about it, or that you've never been to a game?"

"Well, no."

"When you hide the truth about yourself, you're lying. And the moment you lie, you can't feel accepted by the people you're with."

"But if I tell them how little I know about the things they like, they'll think I'm stupid."

"You *are* stupid, at least about sports. We're all stupid about lots of things. Do you feel comfortable around me?"

"Yes."

"But I love sports, just like the men you work with. You feel accepted by me because you chose to tell me the truth about yourself. If you had lied to me, you wouldn't feel comfortable around me, either."

"But if I tell the truth to the guys at work," Andrew said, "they might not accept me like you have."

"That's true. Some of them might not. On the other hand, as long as you lie to them, you won't ever feel accepted by *any* of them."

We can only feel loved when people accept us as we really

are. They can't do that until *we* tell the truth and allow them to see us. The only way to overcome our fear of telling the truth about ourselves is simply to do it. On the other hand, we don't have to tell people everything about ourselves, and we don't have to start with the people we fear most, such as our boss and some family members, to give just a couple of examples.

When Others Lie to Us

People lie to us for the same reasons we lie to them. Their primary intent is not to cause us harm but to get Imitation Love and protect themselves. But when people lie, they always feel more empty and miserable. As we lovingly help people see their lies, we therefore create opportunities for them to feel accepted and loved.

Unfortunately, however, we rarely confront people about their lies for *their* benefit. When people lie, we tend to feel offended or betrayed, so we confront them with the truth to protect *ourselves* or because it gives *us* a sense of power over them. When we tell people the truth without being unconditionally loving, or when they're not capable of hearing the truth about themselves, we can only hurt them, and we need to keep our observations to ourselves.

But even on the occasions when we are loving, it's often useful to remember that telling the truth about *ourselves* can be a good way to respond to all Getting and Protecting Behaviors. Martha learned this as she spoke to her good friend, Beth.

As they were eating lunch, Martha noticed that Beth was unusually quiet. "You seem upset," Martha said.

"I'm really mad at my boss," Beth admitted. "No matter what I do, he finds something wrong with it. Today he filed a written complaint about me, and I could lose my job if he does that again. It's completely unfair, because none of it was my fault."

Martha had known Beth a long time, and she knew that Beth often acted like a victim and blamed the people around her instead of being responsible for her own laziness and bad attitude—on the job or anywhere else. Martha loved Beth and accepted her completely, even when she lied about her mistakes, but she also knew that Beth could never change her life until she started telling the truth about herself.

"Sounds bad," Martha said. "This must have been going on for a long time between the two of you."

"Yes, it has. He's always had something against me."

Martha smiled. "Over the years, I myself have had some bosses I just couldn't get along with. And I've learned one thing about all of them. No matter what they did, in every single case *I* always did something—usually a lot of things— that made the situation worse. If the boss wasn't nice to me, for example, I talked about him behind his back. If he told me to do things I didn't agree with, I did what he wanted me to do as slowly as I could, which just made him more angry at me. My bosses may not have been perfect, but I was a big part of the problem every time."

Beth was stunned. She'd obviously expected Martha to sympathize with her and agree that her boss was a monster. After several seconds of silence, Martha continued by giving even more examples of her selfishness as an employee, show-ing how she had caused tension between herself and her em-ployers and co-workers. The more Martha talked, the more relaxed Beth became.

Beth put up her hands as she spoke. "Okay, okay, I get the point. I haven't been the model employee. I don't like my boss one bit, and I haven't exactly hidden that fact."

She then began to talk about the many things she'd done

to make her boss's job more difficult, and as she did that, she saw how *she* had caused her own problems at work. After several further conversations with Martha, Beth apologized to her boss for all the trouble she'd caused over the past several months. He was naturally surprised and pleased by her honesty, and their relationship improved considerably.

We can all learn how to lovingly help people see the truth about their lies, and one way to do that is to tell them the truth about ourselves. Obviously, the first requirement is that we ourselves feel loved.

> As we tell the truth about ourselves, we give others the courage to do the same and the opportunity to feel unconditionally loved by us.

When We Attack Others

Any time we attempt to motivate people through fear to do what we want, we're attacking them, and we use anger to do that so often that we accept it as normal. Unfortunately, with our anger we make ourselves miserable and destroy our relationships. In the following story, Edward illustrates the effectiveness of telling the truth about himself, which is just a variation on the Be Wrong step we discussed earlier.

Edward was irritated at his wife, Amanda, as he talked to his wise friend. "Everywhere we go, she's late," Edward said. "It's so rude."

"Do *you* ever make mistakes?" asked the wise man.

"Sure, but I'm not late all the time."

"Although you may be perfect about being on time, you do have other faults that unavoidably inconvenience people on occasion, probably more often than you realize. And that's how it has to be. We must be allowed to make our own mistakes. That's how we learn. Does Amanda have the same right you do to make mistakes?"

There was a long pause. "I never thought about that."

As Edward began to see the selfishness of his anger, his irritation faded. It's difficult to stay angry and blaming when we see how unloving we're being.

"So what do I do about Amanda being late?" Edward asked.

"Do you want to divorce her over this?"

"No."

"Then you only have two choices left: live with it and like it or live with it and hate it. You can accept her and love her *while she continues to be late,* **or** you can keep being angry at her. If you choose to accept her, you'll have a loving relationship with a delightful woman who also happens to be late on some occasions. If you choose to resent her, you can only be unhappy. So what's your choice, to be happy or unhappy?"

"You make it sound like such an easy decision."

"It is."

"I want to be happy, obviously, but does that mean she gets to keep being late?"

"Of course. She gets to learn the same way you do—by making mistakes. And it's impossible to make mistakes without inconveniencing other people—in this case, *you*. But if you genuinely care about her happiness, her being late will matter very little to you. Right now, however, your anger demonstrates that you don't feel loved enough to genuinely care about her happiness. You care more about your own convenience, and that's natural until you feel more loved."

As Edward felt accepted, he saw the truth of what his friend was saying.

Blaming and anger protect us from feeling helpless but

never make us feel loved or happy. What we really need is to tell the truth about ourselves and create opportunities to be unconditionally accepted and loved. As we feel loved, we lose our emptiness and fear, along with the anger that is only a re-action to those feelings.

Several days after that conversation, Edward called his friend again and said, "Amanda was late again. I know it's selfish, but I'm still angry about it."

"I was angry most of my life," said his friend, "but I learned to tell the truth about myself and found people who accepted me. As I felt loved, my expectations and anger gradually disap-peared. The same will happen for you. And right now you're doing the best thing you could be doing—you're telling the truth about your own selfishness. How does that feel?"

"I don't think I've ever felt accepted by someone while I was admitting that I was selfish and stupid. I like this."

Edward had felt unloved all his life, and each time his wife was late, he saw her lateness as more evidence that nobody cared about him. His anger gave him some relief from the feel-ing of being alone and helpless. Notice that Edward took four of the five steps to eliminating anger and conflict. He didn't vent his anger at his wife (Be Quiet); instead he remembered that anger was wrong (Be Wrong) and that he had a wise friend who cared about him (Feel Loved). He then called that friend to get even more of the love he needed (Get Loved).

When Others Attack Us

After a shower, Edward left the bathroom a mess, and Amanda was angry about it. As she nagged him, his first im-pulse was to attack her by describing all the times she'd made messes herself. And then he thought about just leaving the room and refusing to talk to her (running). He'd had consid-erable experience using both approaches. But this time he remembered a conversation he'd had with his wise friend during which he'd admitted that defending himself had never made him happy.

Edward knew he couldn't speak to Amanda at that moment without saying something unkind, so he decided to keep quiet and simply said, "Excuse me, I have to go and make a phone call. But I'll be right back to finish this discussion with you." Edward then called his wise friend so that he could feel loved himself. Although he left the room, as he'd done in the past, this time he wasn't running because his motivation was to get love and guidance, not to withdraw from pain.

"Amanda is yelling at me," Edward said, "and I don't know what to do. Instead of blowing up at her and getting into a big fight, I stopped what I was doing to call you."

"You're getting pretty smart," said the wise man. "You already know you can't demand that *she* change in any way. That never works. But there is something you can do that involves only you. You can tell the truth about yourself."

"About what? That I'm feeling unappreciated and angry?"

"Yes. Let's start with *angry*. It's important that you feel accepted *while* you're angry. But as you know, expressing your anger to Amanda wouldn't work very well. I don't think she'd be ready to accept you expressing your anger right now."

"That's why I called you."

"Very wise. How are you feeling at this moment compared with when you were talking to Amanda?"

"Well, I do feel less angry than when Amanda was yelling at me."

"Now let's talk about something a little harder. You said you were feeling 'unappreciated.' When Amanda attacked you, you became afraid, and after that you immediately began to protect yourself, at least in your head. It's easy to see that anger is one of the Protecting Behaviors—it's attacking. But it may not be as easy to see what Protecting Behavior you were using when you mentioned the word *unappreciated*. Do you see it?"

Edward frowned. "Actually, I think I do see it, but I don't like it much. I was being a victim, wasn't I?"

"Of course you were. Don't feel ashamed about it. Just see the truth of it. Now don't stop there. If you were attacking with anger and also acting like a victim—even though it was just silently this time—what is the likelihood that you were feeling loving toward Amanda?"

"Zero?"

"Exactly. You were being angry and unloving toward your own wife. It doesn't get much more selfish and ugly than that. And yet here you are being absolutely honest about it, something very few people on the planet can do. I think you're amazing. How do you feel now?"

"I'd rather spend the rest of the day talking to you than go back and talk to Amanda."

"Take all the time you need. When you feel loved enough, you can go back and tell the truth about yourself to Amanda instead of getting into another useless argument. You won't believe what a relief it is just to say you were wrong."

"But all I did was leave a little mess in the bathroom. Does that justify her yelling at me?"

The wise man laughed. "No, it doesn't, but we're not here to talk about her, just you. Do you want to blame her and have an argument or do you want to learn how to be loving and happy? It seems to me that you already know how to blame and argue. Why not learn something new?"

"Good point."

"Was it thoughtless of you to leave a mess in the bathroom?"

"Well, yes, but—"

The wise man interrupted. "There is no *but*. It's just a fact that in that moment you were thoughtless and selfish. That doesn't make you a bad person, but you can't become happy or have a loving relationship until you accept what you did. You only resist it because the people in your life have always loved you less when you made mistakes like this. But I won't love you less. So face this one small truth: If you really cared about Amanda, you wouldn't have left that mess in the bathroom—true?"

"I guess so."

"Now if you feel loved enough, go and tell the truth to Amanda."

"Actually, I think I can do that. It helped a lot that I could talk to you and feel accepted before I talked to her."

"Oh, I know. I had to do this with friends a million times before I stopped arguing with my wife. But now we don't argue about anything anymore. And it's a lot more fun this way, I can tell you."

Edward told Amanda he'd been thoughtless and wrong. She was dumbfounded and responded by apologizing for having been so unkind toward him. It was a turning point in their relationship.

People are only angry because they're empty and afraid. When we defend ourselves, they feel even more afraid and use their Protecting Behaviors more vigorously. And on it goes. We can, however, stop the vicious cycle simply by telling the truth about ourselves, because when one or both parties in a disagreement admit to being wrong, it's difficult to continue the argument. And as we practice telling the truth and feeling loved, we can actually be loving toward the people who are attacking us.

Sometimes people criticize us without overt anger, but it can still be attacking. It's certainly possible to offer loving criticism, but often when we criticize someone, we do it to protect ourselves or to achieve a sense of importance and power.

When Becky called her parents to describe the house she'd just purchased, her father responded by telling her about the many mistakes she'd made: Property values were declining in that neighborhood, the interest rate on her bank loan was too high, the house was too old, and on and on.

Becky felt stupid and unloved, as she always had as a child, and her impulse was to act like a victim or to get angry at her father for not accepting her, but instead she called a wise friend who encouraged her to tell the truth about herself. Becky admitted to her friend that she didn't know much about real estate and had made several mistakes in the process of buying her house. She also acknowledged that she still felt unsure of being loved, and that in that condition, almost any criticism was very threatening to her. But she knew that was *her* problem, not her father's. As she told the truth about herself, she felt accepted and loved by her wise friend, and her anger vanished.

When people criticize us unkindly—which is in itself a Protecting Behavior—we tend to protect ourselves with Protecting Behaviors of our own, which is foolish, because we can never feel loved and happy when we use these behaviors. Ironically, real safety can be achieved only when we abandon Getting and Protecting Behaviors and simply tell the truth about ourselves, especially about our mistakes and weaknesses.

When we feel loved, we can see unloving criticism for what it is—an attempt by a frightened person to protect himself from further emptiness and fear. We can then accept that person instead of defending ourselves. Becky's father was not

being intentionally malicious. He just didn't feel unconditionally loved himself, and he had learned over the years that
he felt temporarily less worthless and alone when he appeared
to know a lot and offered advice. Unfortunately, his approach
was always condescending and critical, so that instead of in-
gratiating himself with another person as he hoped to do, he
only alienated himself further. But as Becky felt more loved
herself, she was able to accept and love her father even while
he was being critical of her.

When People Act Like Victims

Victimhood is the result of our belief that other people have
an obligation to make choices that will benefit us. It's a combination of anger (that we're not getting as much as we think
we should) and fear (that we'll be hurt).

The cry of the victim is "Look what you did *to* me," as well
as "Look what you should have done *for* me." Victims assume
that the first choice of every other human being should be to
give them what they want. When that doesn't happen, life, as
far as they're concerned, is unfair.

Lori and Phil had been married for ten years and had two
children. On one occasion, typical of many others, Lori said
to Phil, "You never spend any time with me."

"I do things with you all the time," Phil responded, "and
you never appreciate it. Whatever I do, it's never enough."

Both Lori and Phil were acting like victims. Lori believed
that Phil was obligated to satisfy her needs and spend as
much time with her as she wished. Phil believed that Lori
should always appreciate him, never have expectations of
him, and never misunderstand him. They both chose to act
wounded when they failed to get what they expected.

It's difficult to have a relationship with a victim, because
victims see everyone else in the world as doing things *to* them

or *for* them. They see people as *objects* that will either make them happy or hurt them. As a result, they can't have relationships at all, because you can't have a relationship with an object.

Whenever you're acting like a victim or reacting to someone who is, the solution is the same as it is for lying and attacking. You need to tell the truth about yourself, get loved, and love your partner. It's impossible to feel both loved and victimized at the same time.

Lori met two wise friends for lunch and complained that Phil didn't spend enough time with her and wasn't affectionate anymore. These friends knew Lori didn't need sympathy—she needed to be seen clearly and accepted. They told her she was being angry, selfish, and demanding, and because Lori could feel that they accepted and loved her, she listened and admitted she was wrong. It feels wonderful to be accepted while we're doing something wrong.

Over a period of months, Lori continued to tell the truth about herself to wise friends. As she felt more loved, she was eventually able to tell Phil she had been selfish and ungrateful toward him for a long time. Because Phil no longer felt attacked, he stopped withdrawing from her, and their relationship changed dramatically.

When People Run

We run to protect ourselves. When we withdraw physically and emotionally from people, we're running. When we drink alcohol and take drugs, we're running. When Andrew, whom we met earlier in this chapter, failed to tell his co-workers about his lack of interest in sports, he was not only lying, he was also running.

The solution is the same as for all Getting and Protecting

Behaviors. When *we* are running, we need to tell the truth about ourselves and create the opportunity to feel loved and accepted by others. Considerable faith is often required to start that process.

When other people withdraw from us, they're afraid and protecting themselves. When we tell the truth about ourselves and love our partner, we create an atmosphere of trust and the possibility of a connection between us. That doesn't obligate the other person to stop running, but when people feel our willingness to have an honest relationship with them, they're much less likely to feel a need to run from us.

As we tell the truth about ourselves and feel unconditionally loved, the happiness we experience is like nothing else. It makes all the money, power, praise, sex, and other forms of entertainment the world has to offer seem relatively worthless. In addition, as we feel loved ourselves, we can love those around us, and *most* people respond very positively to that and lose their need to use Getting and Protecting Behaviors.

There are, nevertheless, some people who just don't respond positively to being loved. After a lifetime of being hurt, they're just too afraid, and so they continue to protect themselves even when they're being offered what they really need. You, however, will always be happier when you're loved and loving, despite the negative reactions of others. Loving other people is always the happier way to live.

Ending a Relationship (Including Divorce)

Even when we've filled our lives with Real Love and avoided, as best we can, the obstacles to feeling loved and loving others, sometimes there are still some relationships that will end for one reason or another. We need to understand how and why that happens.

Any two people can have a loving relationship if they tell the truth about themselves. Some people, however, are so emotionally crippled by years of feeling empty and afraid that they're either unable or unwilling to tell the truth. If we had unlimited time, we could pursue a relationship with everyone we met. But time is limited and precious, and we naturally want to fill the time we've got with as much knowledge, love, and happiness as we can. That means we must constantly make decisions about establishing, continuing, and ending relationships.

Of course, the people we associate with must be allowed to make their own choices as well, even if they choose to lie, protect themselves, and be miserable. We can still accept these people and care about their happiness, but when someone consistently chooses to lie, he or she can't give or receive Real Love, which is the primary purpose of any relationship. By definition, these people have chosen to not participate in loving relationships, and we may decide that continuing to spend time with them is simply not productive.

If I choose to tell the truth about myself and my friend chooses not to do the same, we are, by definition, walking in different directions and can't possibly have a mutually loving relationship. If I choose to stop associating with that friend, I am, therefore, only accepting *his* decision to go his separate way. It's sometimes better to recognize that an honest relationship does not exist than it is to continue hoping that someone will become what he or she does not wish to be.

I'm *not* suggesting we give up on a relationship as soon as someone tells a lie. Virtually everyone does that occasionally. Nor am I suggesting that we abandon relationships with partners who are not loving us. We all must be in relatively one-sided relationships at one time or other. If it's true that we all need to be loved at times when we have little to give in return, it's equally true that we all need the experience of loving without expectation of reward. That's the definition of unconditional love. When someone habitually refuses to tell the truth, however—especially if that person attacks us and adds to the feelings of emptiness and fear we already have—continuing that relationship may not only be unproductive, it may also interfere with our own ability to tell the truth, feel loved, and learn to love others. For that reason, it's simply best that some relationships end.

We can, however, care unconditionally about another person's happiness and still choose not to spend time with him or her. Joanne discovered this about the relationship she had with two friends.

After learning to tell the truth about herself, Joanne began to feel loved and slowly gained the ability to love other people, but two of her longtime friends wanted nothing to do with telling the truth. They constantly talked about people behind their backs, got angry, acted like victims, and manipulated people for approval. When they did those things with Joanne, who was still unfamiliar with feeling and giving Real Love, she forgot how loved she felt with the wise men and women she'd found, and she became empty and afraid. Then, of course, she resumed using Getting and Protecting Behaviors of her own. When she finally realized that the time she was spending with these friends was making it difficult for her to remain happy, she stopped associating with them. She continued to love them—she genuinely cared about their happiness—but she also knew that her spending time with them was not benefiting either her or them.

How can we know whether a partner will be willing to tell

the truth and participate with us in a loving relationship? If someone isn't willing now, how do we know whether or not he'll be willing to change his mind and try? We can only discover the answers to those questions by continuing to tell the truth ourselves, by loving our partners, and by giving them the opportunity to tell the truth about themselves. Most people resist telling—or even seeing—the truth about themselves in the beginning, and if we abandoned every relationship when our partners lied or protected themselves, we'd have no relationships at all.

If our partner continues to lie consistently, however, it's up to each of us to decide whether it's worth continuing the relationship. How much time and effort do we spend before choosing to give up? We can learn the answer to that question only as we get loved ourselves and learn how to love others. And we learn from making many mistakes.

One winter, I hiked with a friend far out into the desert. Going upstream, we walked and swam many times across a river that ran between the high canyon walls. The water was icy cold, and several times we had to build fires to regain the feeling in our legs.

We'd prepared poorly for our trip. We didn't take sufficient clothing, food, or other supplies. We had no map, and our only instructions came from someone who'd walked downstream in the summertime, when the water was warm. We'd been told, however, that eventually we'd come to a small cabin where we could rest and thaw out.

The hike became a nightmare. In many places, the river was actually frozen over, and we were able to continue only by breaking through the ice with our arms and legs. Our progress was slow and painful, and after pressing on far into the night of the second day, we still hadn't reached the cabin.

By that time, we were hungry, freezing, and out of food. We finally gave up and made camp, exhausted and shivering. It was a miserable night. We slept so close to the fire that we were awakened repeatedly when flames threatened to consume our sleeping bags.

When we awoke the next morning, we couldn't believe what we saw: There was the cabin, across the river less than a hundred yards away. If we'd walked two more minutes the night before, we'd have eaten a hot meal and slept in warm beds!

Similarly, some of us give up on relationships that could have been unspeakably rewarding if we'd just put a little more love and effort into them. How tragic. On the other hand, some relationships cannot be made healthy and need to be abandoned. We're not obligated to spend our lives with every person we meet. We all have to choose where our time will be spent most wisely.

When we understand the importance of telling the truth and sharing Real Love, we can make decisions about spending time with people fairly quickly after meeting them. If a potential partner is manipulative and obviously resists telling the truth about himself, why try to make him into something he isn't? When we meet someone like that, we'd usually be best off moving on to people who are more interested in telling the truth about themselves and finding Real Love.

For more than a year, Jeff had been learning to tell the truth about himself and to feel accepted and loved by a group of wise men. When he told one of these wise friends that he was thinking of marrying Julia, the woman he'd been dating for the last four months, he also expressed some concern. "I'm still inexperienced at judging unconditional love," Jeff said, "especially where women are involved, and I'd value your opinion. How can I be sure Julia is the right woman for me?"

"Are you sleeping with her?" asked his wise friend.

"No. I have learned *some* things from talking with you guys—and from my own experiences."

"That was a good decision. Describe her."

"She's beautiful, intelligent, witty, and has more talents than you can count. We also share lots of interests and have a great time together."

"Do you want to be loved by your spouse or do you want to be entertained by her?"

"No contest. I'd rather be loved."

"Then think about all the positive qualities you listed when I asked you to describe Julia: beautiful, witty, talented, and so on. Is that a description of someone who is unconditionally loving, or someone who would entertain you?"

"Until you asked," Jeff said, "I never thought about it that way. I guess the things I like about her don't have much to do with unconditional love. But I do care about her happiness."

"I believe you. I've known you for more than a year now, and you've learned a lot about feeling loved and caring about other people. But now you also want a relationship with someone who is capable of caring about *you,* don't you?"

"Sure."

"I can't tell you whether this particular woman is the one for you. That's really none of my business, in fact. But I can tell you what I suggest to everyone who is seriously dating and looking for a lifelong partner. If I had to pick the one quality I wanted most in a potential spouse, it would be this: 'Can he or she easily admit being wrong?'"

"Explain that."

"When people can admit they're wrong, it means they can

tell the truth about themselves. If they can do that, they can learn to feel loved and to love other people. People who *can't* admit they're wrong can't learn anything. How can you learn anything if you're already *right* about everything? But if you find someone who can easily admit being wrong, that person can learn just about anything, including how to participate in a mutually loving relationship—and that's what you're looking for, isn't it?"

"Yes."

"So the important question to ask about Julia is this: What happens when she's obviously wrong—like when she's angry? What happens when you disagree about something, like when you don't want to go where she wants or when you don't want to do what she wants to do? Can she admit when she's angry—or wrong?"

Jeff let out a long sigh. "I hadn't really thought about our relationship that way. I was just trying to have a good time. She does have a definite tendency to get irritated, or sulk, when she doesn't get her way. In fact, I usually avoid getting into any kind of conflict with her. I just give in, I'm embarrassed to say."

"Have you talked to her about the things you're learning, like telling the truth about yourself and feeling unconditionally accepted?"

"Yes, but she doesn't seem interested in that stuff. When I talk about my mistakes, either past or present, she seems uncomfortable, and she never talks about hers. She really doesn't like to be wrong. If there's a disagreement, she's always right, and I let her have it her way. But I figured with all her other positive qualities, we could still have a great relationship."

"Have you had other relationships with women who were fun and beautiful like Julia?"

"Sure."

"And did any of those other relationships become what you were looking for in a marriage?"

Jeff smiled. "No, and I'm finally understanding what you're getting at. I was about to make the same mistake with this woman that I made with the others. I even married one of them. It's fun to be with beautiful and talented women, but that kind of excitement never lasts. So what do I do now?"

"Do you think that in the near future, Julia will develop an interest in telling the truth about herself and learning about unconditional love?"

"No, I think she's already made that pretty clear."

"Then if it were me, I'd wave good-bye and run like the wind. Putting off your separation won't benefit either of you. But that's just my opinion. I'm *not* telling you what to do—it's obviously your decision to make."

Jeff didn't need another superficial relationship filled with Imitation Love. He needed more practice telling the truth, feeling loved, and learning to love others. And so he decided to end his relationship with Julia. When he talked to her, he took all the responsibility for the breakup upon himself—he said he simply was not loving enough yet to be in a serious relationship. He didn't blame Julia for anything.

Both Joanne, whom we talked about earlier, and Jeff left relationships they judged were not contributing sufficiently to the Real Love in their lives. That's sometimes a useful approach for many of us to take, but the decision to give up on a relationship should be quite different when we have already made a long-term commitment, as in the case of a spouse or family member.

In a marriage, for example, we've made a commitment to

stay with our partner for a lifetime, even when he or she lies, attacks, acts like a victim, or runs. Marriage provides probably the greatest opportunity any of us will ever have to learn how to love another person. I've seen even truly horrible marriages change as both partners honored their commitment to stay together while they learned to tell the truth and love one another.

However, as we know, a relationship naturally results from the choices made by people independently. And sometimes one or both partners in a marriage make choices that eliminate the possibility of their having a loving relationship.

Cynthia's husband frequently hit her when he was drunk, and he drank almost every day. She lived with that behavior for years, even after she'd had to be hospitalized as a result of her injuries. She eventually decided, however, that she could not learn to tell the truth and find Real Love in that environment.

Having made that decision, she divorced her husband and moved to another city, where she found a group of wise women, learned to tell the truth, and felt the effect of Real Love for the first time in her life. After learning what it feels like to be truly happy, Cynthia eventually married a man who loved her unconditionally. None of her friends had the least doubt that she'd made the right choice in leaving her abusive husband.

Cynthia's decision to leave her marriage may seem obvious, but others are far less clear. Take the case of Michael, whose wife, an angry, bitter woman, had something critical and hateful to say every time she opened her mouth. For many years, Michael tried to please her, but he always failed. Eventually, he became depressed and developed high blood pressure. He felt so attacked and afraid that he couldn't imagine telling the truth about himself or ever being happy.

Michael divorced his wife and moved to another city, where he found a group of wise men, learned to tell the truth, and felt loved for the first time in his life. Like Cynthia, he learned what it felt like to be truly happy, and after a time he married a woman who loved him unconditionally.

Oddly enough, however, most people were not as happy for Michael as they had been for Cynthia, and they accused him of irresponsibly abandoning his wife. Michael's terrible injuries were less evident than Cynthia's, but they were no less painful or deadly. He had never required hospitalization, but his life had been no less threatened.

The point of these stories is not to place blame either on Cynthia's husband or Michael's wife. The lesson to be learned is that neither of these people had ever felt unconditionally loved, and that as a result, they naturally chose to protect themselves and get Imitation Love, which made it impossible for them to have a loving relationship with their spouses. When Cynthia and Michael left their respective marriages, they were accepting the choices their partners had already made not to participate in a loving relationship.

Most people who haven't experienced Real Love find it very difficult to start telling the truth about themselves and so to begin the process of feeling accepted and loved. In a sufficiently hostile environment—as with an angry and manipulative spouse—that learning process can become virtually impossible. The unloving partner may not be *responsible* for his or her spouse's unhappiness, but people who feel unloved do need to find a place where they're not surrounded by accusing and blaming, and where they can feel relatively safe and free to tell the truth. Most people can find such a place without leaving their marriage, but some cannot. Cynthia and Michael decided they could not learn and grow while living with their unloving partners, but that doesn't mean that

Cynthia and Michael were free of responsibility for the failure of those relationships, either.

Abandoning any relationship is not a small thing. Leaving a marriage is a *monumental decision*. Whenever possible, I suggest not making such a decision while we're afraid and protecting ourselves, because under those conditions we can't see anything clearly, and we can't know who or what the real problem is.

If you're empty, angry, offended, blaming, or running, don't make hasty or final decisions. Instead, tell the truth, get loved, and learn to love others first. If Cynthia and Michael had pursued those activities more *before* they left their marriages, those marriages *might* have survived. (Obviously, we can't know that for certain.) When you feel more loved and loving yourself, you'll see clearly and will know the right thing to do with regard to your own marriage.

Before considering a divorce, also ask yourself this: "Have I done all I can do?" That doesn't mean you've got to do all that *anyone* could do, only all that *you* can do. Have you told the truth about yourself to people who accepted and loved you? Have you learned to love others so that you could bring that quality back to your marriage? Or, eager to leave a difficult situation, did you just blame everything on your spouse?

If we don't do all we can to become loving, we'll repeat the same mistakes in our next relationship and will likely fail at that one, too. If we make our present partner responsible for our unhappiness, we'll do that again with the next one. We need to take responsibility for our own feelings and behavior. In most cases, when we leave a committed relationship, we're leaving because *we* are not sufficiently loving ourselves.

Even the most unloving relationships can sometimes change. Sometimes people need to be away from their partner only temporarily, so they can learn more easily in a safer and less confusing environment. Then, when they've learned to tell the truth and feel loved, they can bring that love back to their partner and change the relationship dramatically.

———

In spite of all this talk about leaving relationships, sometimes staying in a relationship with an unloving partner—be it a spouse or a friend—is simply the right thing to do. He or she may never learn to tell the truth, or accept our love, or love us in any way. But we can still learn to love that person and find great happiness in doing that.

The principles in this book are intended to help you take the first steps on your path toward finding and sharing Real Love. The journey never ends. For more information about:

- Greg's seminar and lecture schedule
- engaging Greg as a speaker for your group
- future books and tapes
- past and current journal entries

visit www.GregBaer.com